KETO FAT BOMB

Sweet & Savory Recipes for Ketogenic and Low-carb Diets

(Low-carb Quick Easy & Delicious Keto Fat Bombs Recipes)

Mathew Ralston

Published by Sharon Lohan

© **Mathew Ralston**

All Rights Reserved

Keto Fat Bomb: Sweet & Savory Recipes for Ketogenic and Low-carb Diets (Low-carb Quick Easy & Delicious Keto Fat Bombs Recipes)

ISBN 978-1-990334-20-7

All rights reserved. No part of this guide may be reproduced in any form without permission in writing from the publisher except in the case of brief quotations embodied in critical articles or reviews.

Legal & Disclaimer

The information contained in this book is not designed to replace or take the place of any form of medicine or professional medical advice. The information in this book has been provided for educational and entertainment purposes only.

The information contained in this book has been compiled from sources deemed reliable, and it is accurate to the best of the Author's knowledge; however, the Author cannot guarantee its accuracy and validity and cannot be held liable for any errors or omissions. Changes are periodically made to this book. You must consult your doctor or get professional medical advice before using any of the suggested remedies, techniques, or information in this book.

Table of contents

Part 1 1
Introduction 2
Chapter 1 – Ketogenic Diet In a Nutshell 5
Things to Eat: 11
Things to Eat Occasionally 13
Chapter 2 – Why Fat Bombs? 21
Chapter 3 – Chocolate Flavored Fat Bombs 24
Chocolaty Peanut Butter Fat Bombs 24
Raspberry Bombs 26
Fudgy Keto Bomb 27
Chocolate Creamy Fat Bombs 28
Ice Cream Chocolate Fat Bombs 29
Smoothie Fat Bomb 30
Coconut Fat Bombs 31
Chapter 4 – Keto Fat Bombs with Fruity Flavor 33
Red Fat Bombs 34
Apple Bombs with Caramel 35
Dairy-free Fat Bombs 37
Lemon Flavor Bombs 39
Blueberry Keto Bombs 40
Banana Keto Bombs 42
Caramel Banana Bombs 44
Chapter 5 – Savory and Spicy Fat Bombs 46
Cocoa Fat Bombs with Coffee 47
Peppermint Bombs 49

Pumpkin and Butter Keto Bombs 51
Cinnamon Fat Bombs 53
Lemon Zest Keto Bombs 55
Ginger and Cinnamon Keto Bombs 56
Black Chia Fat Bombs 57
Tahini Keto Bombs 59
Fat Bomb Smoothie 60
Lemon and Avocado Fat Bomb Smoothie 61
Blueberries Keto Smoothie 62
Keto Fudge Bombs 63
Toffee Flavor Fat Bombs 65
Salmon Keto Bombs 66
Chapter 6 – Special Ketogenic Fat Bombs 67
Chocolate Chip Bombs 68
Keto Fudge Squares 70
Chapter 7 - Flavorful Ketogenic Fat Bombs 71
Mini Tarts with Lemon 71
Spicy Cocoa Fat Bombs 73
Pecan Fudge Bombs 74
Flaxseed Fat Bombs 75
Raisins Fudge Bombs 77
Choco Peanut Fat Bombs 78
Butter and Milk Fat Bombs 79
Cereal Fat Bomb 80
Honey and Chocolate Fat Bombs 81
Christmas Fat Bombs 82
Bourbon no bake cookies 83

Oleo Fat Bombs	84
Chocolate Butter Fat Bombs	85
Flaked Coconut Fat Bombs	86
Pudding Fat Bombs	87
Applesauce Fat Bombs	88
Hazelnut Fat Bombs	89
Date Fat Bombs	91
Marshmallow Fat Bombs	93
Samoa Fudge Keto Bombs	95
Conclusion	97
Part 2	98
INTRODUCTION	99
What Is Ketogenic Diet ?	100
What Are The Benefits Of A Ketogenic Diet?	110
What are Fat Bombs?	119
What Are The Benefits Of Fat Bombs?	121
Essential Fat Bomb Ingredients	124
Sweet Fat Bomb Recipes	129
Coconut Berry Delights	129
Fudge Fat Bombs	131
Chocolate Peanut Butter Fat Bombs	133
Caramel Apple Pie Fat Bomb Recipe	135
key lime pie fat bombs	137
Keto Easter Egg Cookie Dough Fat Bombs	139
SEA SALTED CHOCOLATE FAT BOMBS	141
Savoury Fat Bomb Recipes	143
KETO JALAPEÑO POPPERS FAT BOMBS	143

Savory Salmon Fat Bombs 146

Baked Brie and Pecan Prosciutto Savory Fat Bombs............. 148

Breakfast Bacon Fat Bombs 150

Cheesy Pesto Fat Bombs... 152

Savory Pizza Fat Bombs.. 153

BACON, BRAUNSHWEIGER, & PISTACHIO TRUFFLES........... 155

5 Cheese and Bacon Cauliflower Bites.. 157

Savory Mediterranean Fat Bombs 160

Jalapeno Popper Fat Bombs.... **Error! Bookmark not defined.**

Frozen Fat Bomb Recipes .... **Error! Bookmark not defined.**

Coconut Almond Macaroon Fat Bomb Recipe..................... **Error! Bookmark not defined.**

Chocolate Peanut Butter Squares Fat Bomb Recipe .... **Error! Bookmark not defined.**

Frozen Vanilla Mocha Fat Bombs**Error! Bookmark not defined.**

Part 1

Introduction

Obesity is a major problem of the current era because a significant population of the world is suffering from this problem. There are numerous reasons behind overweight and obesity, but we are not going to discuss them. We are writing this book to share possible solutions to obesity. Leptin is a discovery of science for weight regulation. Leptin is a hormone that exists in your fat cells. It is responsible for conveying a message to your brain that you are full. For numerous people, a signal of Leptin is not enough because we are resistant to this hormone.

Before talking more about Leptin, another vital hormone insulin should be discussed. Insulin acts as a master hormone. The level of insulin becomes a signal for other functions and hormones. Insulin is responsible for converting blood sugar into body fat. A diabetic patient with high blood sugar needs a shot of insulin to return it to a reasonable level. Insulin is safe in your fat cells. Body fat becomes a safe place for extra calories. Keep it in mind that high sugar in your blood is dangerous. It may lead to type II diabetes, kidney failure, cancer, fatty liver, blindness, cancer, and loss of limbs.

A healthy person eating 2000 calories and burning 2000 calories on a regular basis will feel good. The insulin shoves 500 of 2000 calories away to your body fat. You have 500 calories as body fat, and you will burn 1500 calories. You will feel hungry, lazy and tired. You are starving effectively so you can get another set of 500 calories for a new insulin shot. 100 out of 500 get stored, and you have to burn only 400. This vicious cycle continues. High insulin depicts the calories to burn instead of stored calories as fat. Now a question arises about the role of leptin. Why it doesn't signal your brain about these fat cells.

The science answer this question in a better way. It is discovered that insulin is blocking leptin receptors. If you eat a diet with high carbohydrates, it will increase your blood sugar that stimulates your pancreases to secrete excessive insulin. The situation will be worse because an excess of insulin can decrease its effectiveness. Insulin brings extra fat to cells, but cells don't need it. They take extra insulin to do their job. It is known as insulin resistance. You have to decrease the insulin secretion by the pancreas. It is possible through brain exercises. Doctors suggest eating less and doing more exercise. The safe and easy way to decrease insulin in the body is to reduce the intake of carbohydrates.

You have to follow a ketogenic diet. This diet requires you to consume moderate protein, high fat and low carb. You may lose the craving for starches and sugar. Ultimately, you will feel better. You are eating less because leptin can do its particular job. Your insulin and blood sugar will drop to a safe level. It is an easy way to feel good, reduce weight and decrease the chances of cancer, fatty liver, kidney failure, blindness, loss of limbs and type II diabetes.

Chapter 1 – Ketogenic Diet In a Nutshell

Ketogenic diet or Keto diet can put your body to nutritional ketosis state. In this state, your body will burn fat for fuel. It can be body fat or the fat that a person eat. If you are eating high-carb foods, your body will rely on glucose for necessary fuel. Some problems are associated with glucose, such as body can store almost 2000 calories related to glucose energy at a time. This energy is stored in the shape of glycogen. After its depletion, you may lose energy and need sugar stat. Extra glucose increases insulin, and this insulin moves glucose into your skeletal cells for burning or storage in the form of glycogen.

It drives glucose in the liver to burn or storage as glucose or convert into fat. The glucose is shipped away in LDL or deposited as foie gras in your liver. Insulin drives glucose into fat cells to transform into fat and store this fat. Fructose (1/2 of table sugar) and the fruit sugar directly goes to the liver to convert into fat. Keep it in mind that corn syrup (high fructose) will be stored as fat instead of burning as energy.

Extra glucose in blood may cause damage, such as it leads to type II diabetes. If you eat moderate protein high-level fats and remove carbs from your diet, insulin level drops because of the presence of less glucose. In this situation, your liver will burn fat to get fuel. Your body is unable to burn its stored fat until the insulin level is low. The ketone is a byproduct of burning fat. These are fatty acids in most cells of human body, such as heart, brain and different other organs. Ketones are directly burned for fuel. Your body is in the state of ketosis doesn't mean that it is okay to burn fat for fuel. It takes almost 3 – 8 weeks to become adapted to fat. Your body will forget the way to deal with glucose efficiently and get more efficient while dealing with stored fat and ketones that originate from burning your body fat.

Once your body is adapted to fat, you will be able to discover constant sources of energy. Your stored body fat will be an excellent source of energy because it doesn't replenish with food. Once your body starts burning fat, it will begin with smooth sailing. You may expect your hunger or cravings to disappear. You can increase the chances of success by eliminating carbs from your diet. By successfully sticking to this routine, you can return to your healthy weight in a short period.

Ketosis

Ketosis state stimulates your liver to break down the stored fat of for fuel. The byproduct of this break down is ketones. Ketone bodies are of three types bet-hydroxybutyrate acid, acetoacetate, and acetone. When your body first time goes into ketosis, you spill ketone acetoacetate. One portion is spontaneously converted into breath ketone (ketones acetone). It is converted into beta-hydroxybutyrate enzymatically. Your brain uses beta-hydroxybutyrate ketone for energy. Portion of fat adaption is becoming better at producing an enzyme beta-hydroxybutyrate dehydrogenase. People often compliant about body odor and bad breath it is normal. It is related to acetone and goes away automatically.

Numerous body cells use ketones for direct energy instead of glucose. However, some cells require glucose, such as parts of the brain, cells in eyes and red blood cells. These parts can get glucose from the liver. The liver is a built-in generator of glucose that uses protein to produce glucose. This procedure is known as gluconeogenesis (gluco means sugar, neo means new, genesis means create). Your liver is responsible for creating novel sugar, just sufficient for the use of vital cells. It is not a magical trick. Human body survives without carbs for thousands of eons.

Who must not follow the ketogenic diet?

A keto diet is safe for everyone, but some groups need special consideration, such as:

- Do you use medicine for diabetes, such as insulin?
- Are you breastfeeding?

- Are you living on the medication of high blood pressure?

If you fall in above three groups, it is essential to consider the advice of your doctor.

Identify If You are in Ketosis

You may measure the ketosis state of your body via blood or urine strips. The urine strips can be inaccurate, and blood strips are costly. Instead, you can consider some physical symptoms that enable you to find out if you are following the perfect track:

Augmented Urination: Keto acts as an ordinary diuretic so you will visit bathroom frequently. A ketone body known as acetoacetate is expelled in urination and lead to unnecessary visits to the bathroom for novices.

Dry Mouth: The excessive urination can make your mouth dry and increase your thirst. Make sure to drink sufficient water and replenish electrolytes (magnesium, potassium, salt).

Bad Breath: A ketone body, acetone, primary excretes in a breath. It may smell sharp like an overripe fruit or nail polish remover. It is temporary and may go away in the long-run.

Increased Energy and Reduced Hunger: After keto flu, you will experience a decreased level of hunger and invigorated mental state.

Instead of worrying about your ketosis, it will be good to focus on a nutritional level. Make sure to eat sufficient food and stay within a particular macro range.

Understand Macros

Macros mean macronutrients that is your regular intake of three major nutrients, such as carbohydrates, protein, and fats. It says 5% of energy comes from carbs, 25% from protein and 70% from fat. Make sure to combine the rule with an essential rule that you should limit to 20g carbs in a day.

Types of Ketogenic Diet

Three types of ketogenic diet allow you to burn your body fat:

- SKD (Standard Ketogenic Diet): A classic diet that everyone follows.

- TKD (Targeted Ketogenic Diet): A variation where you can eat as per standard ketogenic diet, but intake small quantities of fast-digesting carbs before your workout.

- CKD (Cyclical Ketogenic Diet): A variation of keto for contest goers and bodybuilders. It allows you to have a carb for one day in a week and resupply your glycogen stores.

Things to Eat and Avoid

One of the best ways to lose weight is the use of natural and healthy food items and exercise. You have to control your portion size and go for a walk on a regular basis. You have to need to follow the Ketogenic diet. A simple rule of thumb is to eat real food, such as meat, nuts, eggs, yogurt, fruits, and vegetables. You should eat a few things during Ketogenic diet:

Water can Do Wonders

You may often hear that water can help you to shed few pounds, and it is true because of the miraculous properties of water. If you eat fruits and vegetables with water, then you can reduce the body mass and waistline. The water will fill you up to make you eat less amount of food. You have to include at least 90% water in your diet, and it is secure by consuming season fruits and vegetables with water.

Broccoli and Cabbage

Broccoli is an excellent source of fiber and calcium; therefore, you can add it to your salad and soups to shed some extra pounds. The cabbage has antioxidant properties with lots of vitamin C. It can boost your metabolism and trigger weight loss speed. You can pair raw cabbage with apple, orange juice, and chicken to make a yummy and healthy salad.

Things to Eat:

You can eat a few things freely without any tension, such as:

Wild and Grass-fed Animal Sources

Your diet should include grass-fed meat, such as goat, lamb, beef, and venison along with wild fish and seafood. Avoiding farmed fish is a right decision. Pastured poultry, eggs, ghee, gelatin, and butter are also suitable for your diet. These are high in omega-3 fatty acids. You should avoid sausages and meat coated with breadcrumbs, sweet sauces dogs, and starchy sauces.

Healthy Fats

Your diet should contain saturated fats, such as lard, chicken fat, tallow, duck fat, clarified butter, ghee, coconut oil, olive oil and pure butter. You can get monounsaturated fat from macadamia, olive oil, and avocado. For polyunsaturated omega 3s, you can include animal protein in your diets, such as seafood and fatty fish.

Non-starchy Vegetables

Your diet should have leafy greens such as lettuce, spinach, bok choy, swiss chard, chives, radicchio, endive, etc. some cruciferous vegetables are radishes, kale, and kohlrabi. Some bamboo shoots, cucumber, zucchini, asparagus, celery stalk and spaghetti squash will be an excellent addition to your diet.

Fruits

Avocado is an excellent choice for you because it has healthy fats.

Condiments and Beverages

Water, black coffee without cream and sugar (you can use coconut milk), black or herbal tea and lemon water are helpful to reduce weight. Your diet may have sauerkraut, Kombucha, fermented foods, pickles, pesto, homemade bone broth, mustard, low-fat mayonnaise and all herbs and spices. If you want to use whey protein, make sure to check artificial sweeteners, additive, soy lecithin and hormones. Gelatin and protein should be free from hormone so always prefer grass-fed.

Things to Eat Occasionally

A few vegetables, fruits and fats are sometimes allowed while following a Ketogenic diet.

Fruits, Vegetables, and Mushrooms

- *There are some vegetables, such as white, green and red cabbage, broccoli, cauliflower, fennel, Brussels, sprouts, rutabaga, and swede. These are cruciferous vegetables, and you should use them occasionally.*
- *Peppers, eggplants, and tomatoes are some nightshades. Parsley root, onion, spring onion, winter squash, garlic, and leek are root vegetables.*
- *Some sea vegetables are okra, bean sprouts, kombu and nori, French artichokes, wax beans, and snap peas.*
- *You can include berries (strawberries, cranberries, blueberries, mulberries, and cranberries) in your diet, but don't eat them frequently.*
- *Olives, rhubarb, and coconut should not be consumed on a regular basis.*
- *Full-fat Dairy and Grain-fed Protein Sources*

- *You should avoid the regular use of the following food items:*
- *Eggs, poultry, ghee, and beef (Stay away from farmed pork because it is high in omega 6s).*
- *Dairy products include cottage cheese, full-fat yogurt, sour cream, cheese and full-fat cream. Avoid all the goods that labeled "low-fat" because most of these products have starch and sugar.*
- *Beware of added starch and preservatives in bacon. Nitrates are only acceptable to excessive use of antioxidants.*
- *Seeds and Nuts*
- *Macadamia nuts because these are low in carbohydrates and have a high amount of omega 3s.*
- *Almonds, pecans, walnuts, flaxseeds, sesame seeds, pine nuts, hazelnuts, pumpkin seeds, sunflower seeds, sesame seeds and hemp seeds.*
- *If you want to eat Brazil nuts, you should focus on their level of selenium. You should avoid high nuts with high selenium.*

Soy Products (Fermented)

- You can eat fermented products, such as Natto, soy sauce, coconut amino, or Tempeh.

- If you want black soybeans and Edamame beans, try to select unprocessed beans.

Condiments

- Zero-carb sweeteners are suitable, such as Erythritol, Swerve, Stevia, etc.

- Allowed thickeners are xanthan gum (not suitable for paleo diet), arrowroot powder, etc.

- Sugar-free puree, ketchup, and pasta sauce are also allowed.

- Carob and cocoa powder, dark chocolate (extra dark) and cocoa powder are good for the ketogenic diet.

- Stay away from sugar-free mints and chewing gums. You can have some herbs.

Seeds, Fruits, Vegetables, and Nuts with Mediocre Carbohydrates

- Carrot, celery root, parsnip, sweet potato, and beetroot have average carbohydrates.

- Cantaloupe, watermelon, honeydew melons and Galia.

- Cashew nuts, pistachio, and chestnuts.

- Better to Avoid or take only a small amount: dragon fruit, apricot, nectarine, peach, grapefruit, apple, kiwifruit, orange, plums, cherries, figs and kiwi berries.

Alcohol

You should avoid spirits, white wine (dry) and red wine (dry) for weight loss. If you are maintaining your weight instead of losing, you can take a small amount.

Completely Avoid Them

If you want to reduce weight, it is essential to avoid factory –farmed meat, foods high in carbohydrates and any kinds of processed food.

All Grains

You should avoid all grains, such as rye, corn, wheat, oats, rice, millet, bulgur, barley, buckwheat, quinoa, white potatoes, amaranth and sprouted grains. You should stay away from pizza, cookies, pasta, bread, and crackers as well. You can't reduce weight by consuming table sugar, agave sugar, cakes, sweet puddings, ice creams and soft drinks.

Factory-farmed Fish and Pork

Factory-farmed fish and pork are high in omega-6 fatty acids and PCBs. Avoid them to improve your health. Farmed fish may have a significant amount of mercury as well.

Processed Foods

All kinds of processed foods have BPA, MSG, carrageenan (almond milk) and wheat gluten. You should avoid them because you may not get any notification about them on the label.

Artificial Sweeteners

Some artificial sweeteners contain sucralose, acesulfame, aspartame, and saccharin. These can increase your craving and cause other health issues.

Refined Oils and Fats

These are safflower, canola, sunflower, soybeans, corn and grapeseed oil. You should avoid margarine as well because it has trans fats.

Zero-carb, low-carb and low-fat Products

These are diet soda, drinks, chewing gums, mints, Ketogenic products, etc. These may have a high amount of carbs or gluten and artificial additives.

Milk

You are allowed to drink only a small amount of full-fat (raw) milk. It is not recommended because milk can be a burden on your digestive system. It often lacks good bacteria because of pasteurization and may contain hormones. Milk is quite high in carbs because only 100 ml milk has 4 to 5 grams carbs. For tea and coffee, replace milk with a reasonable amount of cream.

Alcoholic and Sugary Drinks

Sweet wine, beer, and cocktails are strongly prohibited; hence, you can try healthy versions of drinks and cocktails.

Tropical Fruits

You are not allowed to eat any tropical fruit, such as papaya, banana, mango, and pineapple. Grapes and tangerine are high in carbs so avoid them as well. You should avoid all kinds of fruit juices; even 100 percent fresh juices are not allowed. You can enjoy vegetable and fruit smoothies. Juices are merely sweet water with no fiber, but smoothies give you fiber. You should avoid dates and raisins as well.

Avoid Soy Products for Health Reasons

For some health reasons, you should stay away from non-GMO fermented food items. You have to keep yourself away from wheat gluten that is often used in low-carb diets. You are not allowed to eat bread and wheat gluten food items. Be careful about BPA-lined cans and try to use original packaging (BPA-free) like glass jars to keep coconut milk, mayonnaise, and ketchup. BPA has lots of adverse effects on your health, such as cancer and thyroid function. You should also avoid sulfites (gelatin and dry fruits), carrageenan (almond milk items) and MSG (whey protein items).

Chapter 2 – Why Fat Bombs?

If your body runs on fat, it is a good idea to add keto fat bombs in your diet. These are energetic snacks to consume before and after a workout. Here are some essential characteristics of keto fat bombs:

- **Small Size:** These are high in fat, so all recipes require you to make them small in size.
- **Healthy Fats:** Coconut butter or coconut oil contains right nutrients. These are staple ingredients while making these recipes.
- **Nuts:** Several recipes include nuts because numerous types of nuts have high-fat content. You have to choose right nuts to get its benefits.
- **Perishable:** Composition of fat bombs require you to put them in fridge or freezer.
-

Fat bombs are good for weight loss. This healthy snack can increase the ability of your body to absorb fat-soluble vitamins, such as vitamin A, vitamin E and vitamin D.

The keto bombs are made with olives and peanuts to decrease your bad (LDL) cholesterol and increase good (HDL) cholesterol.

They have the ability to decrease the speed of digestion and break down carbohydrates into sugar to keep the sugar level of your blood stable. This procedure will keep you full for a more extended period. You can avoid overeating and binge eating.

The coconut oil is utilized in keto fat bombs that is an excellent ingredient to accelerate weight loss. You must avoid the eschew of coconut oil.

Essential Ingredients

The fat bombs are made of three essential ingredients, such as flavoring, healthy fats, and texture.

Healthy Fats

You can add coconut cream, coconut milk, coconut oil, almond butter, coconut butter, cacao butter, cultured ghee, avocado oil, butter or bacon fat.

Flavoring

Spices, peppermint extract, salt, cacao powder, dark chocolate (100%), and vanilla extract (sugar-free).

Texture

Shredded coconut, bacon bits (sugar-free), chia seeds, walnuts, pecans, almond and cacao nibs.

Simple Steps:

- Mix all ingredients in a food processor mixing bowl. If you are using a solid fat, you can put it over the stove or in the microwave.

- Make small fat balls, or pour the blend into the muffin cup, or spread on a baking pan.

- Put in the freezer or fridge for numerous hours to make mixture solid. If you are using one baking pan, you can cut into slices.

Chapter 3 – Chocolate Flavored Fat Bombs

There is no need to compromise over your love for chocolate. Here are some delicious and healthy recipes tomake fat bombs at home.

Chocolaty Peanut Butter Fat Bombs

Chocolate and peanut butter can do wonder without sugar. You can try them at home.

Cooking Time: 30 minutes

Servings: 24

Ingredients

- 4 tablespoons pasture butter
- 4 tablespoons peanut butter, without sugar
- 4 tablespoon cocoa powder, without sugar
- Any Sweetener, 1 packet
- 8 tablespoons coconut oil, extra virgin
- 24 plastic molds, cup size

Instructions:

1. Transfer oil, pasture, and peanut butter in a container that can be kept in the microwave on high heat for almost 35 seconds.
2. Melt it and then beat to make it smooth. It is time to include sweetener and cocoa powder and beat to make a blend.
3. Take 24 molds and equally pour the mixture, and it is time to keep it in the refrigerator for almost 30 minutes. If you want to store it in the freezer, then use a zip lock bag.

Raspberry Bombs

Chocolate and raspberry will be an ideal combination for everyone. You will really like this delicious and yummy dessert.

Cooking Time: 2 hours

Servings: 15

Ingredients

- Coconut oil 5 tablespoons
- Raspberry syrup 2 tablespoons, free from sugar
- Butter 5 tablespoons
- Cocoa powder 2 tablespoons

Instructions:

1. Take a pan and add all ingredients one by one to cook on a low heat. You need a consistent chocolate sauce.
2. Add in the mold and let it freeze for almost 2 hours. Enjoy frozen fat bombs after taking them out of the mold.

Fudgy Keto Bomb

A sweet combination of cocoa powder and macadamia.

Cooking Time: 10 minutes

Servings: 15

Ingredients

- *2 oz Butter (you can choose anyone, but the cocoa butter is better for you)*
- 2 Tablespoons cocoa powder, without sugar
- 2 Tablespoons Sweetener
- 4 oz Macadamias (chopped)
- ¼ cup coconut oil

Instructions:

1. Liquefy the cocoa butter in a cooking pan with water and now add cocoa in the pan. Now add sweetener and blend all the ingredients well.
2. It is time to add macadamias and cream. Mix well and keep it on the flame.
3. Once you get a smooth blend, now add the molds in the candy cups made of papers and let them cool on a room temperature.
4. You need to keep in the refrigerator to make them hard.

Chocolate Creamy Fat Bombs

Coconut and butter can do wonder in your ketogenic diet.

Cooking Time: 10 minutes

Servings: 24

Ingredients

- 8 oz almond butter
- Small pack of butter with salt
- 8 oz coconut oil
- Chocolate, 1 Stick

Instructions:

1. The coconut oil, almond and salted butter will be added in a bowl to keep in microwave for a few seconds.
2. Now divide this melted mixture into 24 cupcakes. Let it cool in the freezer and then melt the chocolate stick and 2 tablespoons of butter.
3. Now mix both the blends and equally divide among 24 cupcakes. Keep in the refrigerator to make the solid.

Ice Cream Chocolate Fat Bombs

Enjoy chilled fat bombs with whipping cream and protein powder.

Cooking Time: 10 minutes

Servings: 20

Ingredients

- 1 cup spread, (whipped and peanut flavor)
- 1 cup sweetener, granulated
- 1 cup chocolate whipping cream
- 3 scoops of your favorite protein powder

Instructions:

1. Take a mixing bowl, pour chocolate cream, and beat it well. You can use an electric mixture to use on low speed.
2. Now you need to add the protein powder and sweetener and keep mixing the blend. Grease a muffin tin and place a liner on each hole.
3. Distribute the mixture evenly into the tins and place in the refrigerator to serve chilled.

Smoothie Fat Bomb

Simple recipe for smoothie like fat bombs for people of all ages.

Cooking Time: 10 minutes

Servings: 2

Ingredients

- 2/3 cups berries
- Whey protein, 1 scoop
- ¼ cup water
- 1 cup chocolate milk
- 2 egg yolks, raw only

Instructions:

1. It is very simple, just take a full-size cup, blend all the ingredients and add crushed ice.
2. You are done to enjoy your favorite chocolate bombs.

Coconut Fat Bombs

Coconut oil and cocoa powder allows you to make delicious treat for your diet.

Cooking Time: 10 minutes

Servings: 15

Ingredients

- 2 tablespoons cocoa powder, free from sugar
- 1 tbsp Heavy cream
- 1 tablespoon sweetener
- 1/4 cup Coconut oil
- 24 almonds, crushed
- 2 tablespoons peanut butter, salty is good

Instructions:

1. Chop almonds and sprinkle on a container lined with baking paper. Mix coconut oil and powder to make them smooth. You can melt the coconut oil if needed.
2. Pour artificial sweetener and cream to make a smooth blend. Sprinkle chocolate in the baking pan over almonds and spread it evenly.
3. Keep the container in your freezer for almost 10 minutes. Use a knife to spread butter on the top of hard mixture and then keep it in the freezer again.

4. Once it is chilled, remove the cooking paper and cut the even pieces of the chocolate.

Chapter 4 – Keto Fat Bombs with Fruity Flavor

You can increase the healthiness and taste of fat bombs by adding some fruits in the recipe. See this section.

Red Fat Bombs

Cooking Time: 2 hours

Servings: 15

Ingredients

- 1/2 cup strawberries
- 1/4 cup coconut oil
- 3/4 cup soft cream cheese
- 2 tablespoons stevia, liquid
- 1 vanilla bean or extract

Instructions:

1. Chop cheese and butter to mix them together in a bowl. Keep it at room temperature for 30 to 60 minutes to get a soft mixture.
2. Rinse all the strawberries and detach green parts. Keep them in a bowl and use a fork to blend them well for a smooth mixture. It is time to add vanilla and stevia to mix them well in the strawberries.
3. Add the rest of the ingredients as well and then add this mixture in soft butter and cheese. Beat it properly either with a manual mixture or electric processor. Equally divide the mixture in the muffin molds and keep in the freezer for 2 hours.
4. Once they become hard, take out of the mold and store in a container to enjoy anytime. You should store this container in a freezer.

Apple Bombs with Caramel

Have a pinch of caramel and apple in your fat bombs. See this delicious recipe.

Cooking Time: 10 minutes

Servings: 15

Ingredients

- 2 green apples, medium sized, chopped after peeling (you can keep unpeeled as per your preference)
- 2 tablespoons coconut oil
- 1 teaspoon cinnamon, powder
- 5.4 oz cream (coconut flavor)
- 1/2 cup butter, coconut flavor
- 20 drops sweetener, toffee flavor
- Salt as per taste

Instructions:

1. Take a cooking pan to cook apple with coconut oil and make them soft. It is time to add cinnamon in apples and mix them well.
2. Now use a powerful blender to make a smooth mixture of apples. It is time to add sweetener and coconut cream.

3. Distribute this mixture in plastic molds and keep in the refrigerator. The size and shape of the molds will be based on your own choice.
4. Serve them chilled after they become hard. You can store these balls in the freezer.

Dairy-free Fat Bombs

If you are on a vegan or dairy-free diet, you can try this recipe for healthy fat bombs.

Cooking Time: 10 minutes

Servings: 12

Ingredients

- ½ cup coconut oil
- 1 teaspoon vanilla
- ¼ cup cream, coconut flavor
- ½ cup Fruity Chocolate bar
- 2 teaspoon cocoa powder
- 8-16 drops sweetener or honey
- Organic seed butter
- 12 plastic cups for cakes

Instructions:

1. Take a small saucepan to mix all the ingredients, but don't add seed butter. Let the ingredients melt with a slow heat, but make sure to avoid microwave for melting process.

2. Blend all the ingredients and equally distribute in the plastic cakes to keep in the freezer for 10 minutes.
3. After 10 minutes, remove from the refrigerator and then add a small amount of seed butter on the top of each cup.
4. Keep it in the freezer to make them harder, then remove from the cups, and store in a plastic container in the freezer. On the room temperature, the fat may start to melt.

Lemon Flavor Bombs

Lemon can add a unique flavor and taste to your fat bombs. Try these bombs.

Cooking Time: 10 minutes

Servings: 15

Ingredients

- 4 tablespoons butter
- 2oz cheese cream
- 4 tablespoons whipping cream
- 1 fresh lemon, juice
- 1 tsp lemon extract (but you can also choose vanilla)
- Sweetener or honey

Instructions:

1. You need to prepare a few plastic molds with baking paper (foil liner). Heat the cream cheese and add oil and butter to beat them well.
2. Add juice of one lemon, but throw the seeds away. Add extracts and sweetener as per your taste. Carefully pour this mixture in the molds and keep in the freezer for the whole night.
3. In the morning, remove from the molds and secure in a plastic bag.

Blueberry Keto Bombs

Cooking Time: 10 minutes

Servings: 15

Ingredients

1 small cup blueberries

4 oz butter

3/4 cup healthy coconut oil

Sweetener as per taste

4 oz soft cream cheese

¼ cup cream (coconut flavor)

Instructions:

1. Use whole berries or make a puree with these ingredients to get a perfect blend. Take a plastic ice-cube tray and distribute the blend in the plastic tray. You can freeze them to get hard bombs.
2. Puree can be made by blending all the ingredients in a food processor to get a smooth puree.
3. Whole berries: if you want to add whole berries, then put 3 to 4 berries in each mold and add a blend of melted butter, coconut oil, cream and the rest of the ingredients on the top of whole berries.
4. Let the bombs become hard by keeping this tray in the refrigerator.

Nutrition Facts
- *Calories 185*
- *Total Fat 19.9g*
- *Total Carbohydrate 1.9g*
- *Protein 0.7g*

Banana Keto Bombs

Cooking Time: 2 hours

Servings: 16

Ingredients

- 1/2 cup strawberries and Banana
- 1/4 cup coconut oil
- 3/4 cup soft cream cheese
- 2 tablespoons stevia, liquid
- 1 vanilla bean or extract

Instructions:

1. Chop cheese and butter to mix them together in a bowl. Keep it at room temperature for 30 to 60 minutes to get a soft mixture.
2. Rinse all the strawberries and detach green parts. Keep strawberries and banana in a bowl and use a fork to blend them well for a smooth mixture.
3. Now add vanilla and stevia to mix them well in the strawberries. Add the rest of the ingredients as well and then add this mixture in soft butter and cheese. Beat it properly either with a manual mixture or electric processor.
4. Equally divide the mixture in the muffin molds and keep in the freezer for 2 hours. After they become hard, take out of the mold and store in a container

to enjoy anytime. You should store this container in a freezer.

Caramel Banana Bombs

Get three delicious flavors "coffee, caramel and banana" in these bombs.

Cooking Time: 40 minutes

Servings: 15

Ingredients

- 30 ml coffee
- 200 ml egg whites
- 40 g protein powder (your favorite flavor)
- 15 ml caramel syrup
- 1 banana slices
- 1 tablespoon yogurt, fat-free
- 30 ml almond milk, without sugar (you can take chocolate flavor)

Instructions:

1. Heat an oven in advance at 450°F. Take a bowl and mix egg whites, protein, and buckwheat and blend in a food processor for 60 seconds. Take a bread pan and spread the batter evenly to microwave for 1 minute.
2. Mix the content and keep it on the side after one minute. Now add caramel syrup, yogurt, coffee and almond milk a blender to blend for 1 minute.

3. Pour this mixture in the bread pan and mix before pouring into the muffin cups. Top with the chopped bananas and keep in oven for 20 to 25 minutes.

Chapter 5 – Savory and Spicy Fat Bombs

If you are tired of eating sweet keto bombs, you can try these recipes with some spicy flavors.

Cocoa Fat Bombs with Coffee

Cooking Time: 10 minutes

Servings: 15

Ingredients

- Butter, 4 tablespoons
- Coconut oil, 4 tablespoons
- Whipping cream, 2 tablespoons
- Cocoa powder without sugar, 1 tablespoon
- Coffee, you only need extract, ½ teaspoon
- 4 tablespoons sugar
- 1 pinch or more black pepper, as per taste

Instructions:

1. Melt the butter and then add cream in it. Mix well and keep it on one side to let it cool down.
2. Make a blend of cocoa powder, oil, black pepper, sweetener and extract of coffee. Blend the mixtures of both the bowls and then blend them well with a stick. Keep the small molds on a baking sheet and pour almost a tablespoon of batter in each mold.
3. Keep these molds in the freezer with baking sheet and let them settle for 20 minutes. If you want to

make the pops, then add the sticks in the middle of the bombs before they become too hard.
4. Keep in the refrigerator again making them harder and then storing in a plastic bag in a freezer for later use.

Peppermint Bombs

These bombs will look good and taste great with peppermint extract.

Cooking Time: 10 minutes

Servings: 12

Ingredients

- ¾ cup butter, melted (better to use coconut flavor)
- ½ teaspoon peppermint extract
- 2 tablespoons cocoa powder
- 1/3 cup coconut, shredded
- 3 tablespoons oil, (better to use coconut oil in melted form)

Instructions:

1. Mix butter, coconut, 1 tablespoon oil and peppermint extracts to get an even blend. Keep the small molds on a baking sheet and pour almost 1/2 tablespoon of batter in each mold.
2. Keep these molds in the freezer with baking sheet and let them settle for 20 minutes.
3. Mix remaining 2 tablespoons of coconut oil and cocoa powder to pour it into the molds kept in the refrigerator.

4. Remove the molds from the refrigerator and pour cocoa blend in each mold. Keep it back in the refrigerator to get hard bombs.
5. You can store these bombs in the freezer, but take out of freezer almost 5 minutes before serving.

Pumpkin and Butter Keto Bombs

Get a unique flavor of ginger, clove and pumpkin with these keto bombs.

Cooking Time: 30 minutes

Servings: 15

Ingredients

- 2 tablespoons coconut oil
- Pasture butter, ½ stick is enough
- Cinnamon and nutmeg
- 1/2 cup pumpkin
- Ground Clove: ½ teaspoon
- Ground Ginger: ½ teaspoon
- Sweetener: 4 tablespoons

Instructions:

Melt the butter and coconut oil to mix them well.

Make a blend of pumpkin, sweetener and all spices to get a smooth mixture. Keep the small molds on a baking sheet and pour almost a tablespoon of batter in each mold.

Keep these molds in the freezer with baking sheet and let them settle for 10 minutes. After 10 minutes, take out the bombs from the mold and roll them to make balls.

Keep in the refrigerator again making them harder and then storing in a plastic bag in a freezer for later use.

Cinnamon Fat Bombs

Cinnamon and grated ginger will give a unique flavor to these fat bombs.

Cooking Time: 20 minutes

Servings: 12

Ingredients

- 8 ounces cheese cream, soft and full fat
- 1 teaspoon grated ginger
- ½ cup sweetener for baking
- ½ teaspoon cloves, powder
- ½ teaspoon nutmeg, powder
- 1 teaspoon cinnamon
- ¾ cup oil, coconut is better to use

Instructions:

1. Slowly process all the ingredients one by one in the food processor, but don't pour coconut oil and cheese.
2. After blending all the ingredients, you can slowly pour the coconut oil and cream cheese. Turn the mixture into small balls and keep in the refrigerator for 15 minutes.
3. Dab the top with melted chocolate after 15 minutes and keep them again in the refrigerator. You need

to make them harder and then store in a plastic bag in a freezer for later use.

Lemon Zest Keto Bombs

Flavor these keto bombs with lemon zest and juice. Serve chilled.

Cooking Time: 20 minutes

Servings: 15

Ingredients

- Coconut oil, ¼ cup (measure after melting it)
- Pasture butter, 4 tablespoons
- Lemon zest, ½
- Lemon juice, 1 tablespoon
- Sweetener, 2 tablespoons
- 4 oz cheese cream, soft

Instructions:

1. Use a hand mixer to blend the ingredients and then pour this mixture into the cupcake molds evenly.
2. Keep these molds in the freezer for the whole night to make them harder and then store in a plastic bag in a freezer for later use.

Ginger and Cinnamon Keto Bombs

Cooking Time: 30 minutes

Servings: 12

Ingredients

- 1 teaspoon grated ginger
- 1/2 teaspoon cinnamon
- ¾ cup oil, coconut is better to use
- 1 cup coconut milk and butter, separately 1 cup each
- *Sweetener*
- Shredded coconut, 1 cup

Instructions:

1. Slowly melt all the ingredients one by one, but don't pour shredded coconut. After melting all the ingredients, you can slowly pour the shredded coconut and mix them well.
2. Turn the mixture into small balls and keep in the refrigerator for 15 minutes. Dab the top with melted chocolate after 15 minutes and keep them again in the refrigerator.
3. You need to make them harder and then store in a plastic bag in a freezer for later use.

Black Chia Fat Bombs

Black chia can be a good addition in your diet to keep your healthy and energetic.

Cooking Time: 30 minutes

Servings: 12

Ingredients

- 3 tablespoons black seeds of chia
- ½ cup coconut flakes, without sugar
- 2 tablespoons coconut flour
- 2 tablespoons butter, natural peanut butter
- ½ cup heavy cream will be used in two parts
- 10 packet sweetener
- 1 tablespoon oil
- ¼ teaspoon, maple flavor
- Pumpkin spice, ½ teaspoon

Instructions:

1. Take a saucepan and blend heavy cream and sweetener, let them heat on a medium heat to get bubbles. Remove from heat and let it cool down. Now mix maple flavor, pumpkin spice, peanut butter, heavy cream and keep it aside.

2. Toast flour, chia and flakes in a separate bowl and then mix these and the rest of the ingredients in the mixing bowl.
3. Pour this mixture into the cupcake molds evenly. Keep these molds in the freezer to let them harden and then store in a plastic bag in a freezer for later use.

Tahini Keto Bombs

Make these delicious bombs with Tahini paste and walnuts.

Cooking Time: 30 minutes

Servings: 12

Ingredients

- Coconut oil, 1/2 cup
- Cocoa powder without sugar, 2 tablespoons
- Granulated sweetener, 1 tablespoon
- 2 tablespoons walnut
- Tahini paste, 1 tablespoon

Instructions:

1. Melt the coconut oil and add all the ingredients. Leave for some time to let them cool, but start working before the mixture starts settling down.
2. Keep the small molds on a baking sheet and pour almost a tablespoon of batter in each mold. Keep these molds in the freezer with baking sheet and let them settle for 20 minutes.
3. After 20 minutes, pop the walnut in the middle. Keep in the refrigerator again to make them harder and store in a plastic bag in a freezer for later use.

Fat Bomb Smoothie

You can make delicious smoothie with the fat bomb. See this great recipe.

Cooking Time: 10 minutes

Servings: 2

Ingredients

- Almond milk, 1 cup
- 2 tablespoons crushed almonds
- 1/3 cup strawberries
- One pinches salt

Instructions:

1. Take a food processor and make a blend of all these ingredients to make a delicious smoothie.
2. Serve chilled by keeping in the refrigerator.

Lemon and Avocado Fat Bomb Smoothie

Avocado and lemon has numerous benefits that you can enjoy in this recipe.

Cooking Time: 10 minutes

Servings: 2

Ingredients

- ½ cup water
- ¼ cup ice
- Lemon Juice, one to two lemons
- ½ cup coconut milk
- 5 tablespoons avocado
- 3 egg yolks

Instructions:

1. Take a food processor and make a blend of all these ingredients to make a delicious smoothie.
2. Serve chilled by keeping in the refrigerator.

Blueberries Keto Smoothie

Use fresh blueberries and almond milk to make these great fat bombs.

Cooking Time: 10 minutes

Servings: 2

Ingredients:

- Almond milk, 1 cup
- 2 tablespoons crushed almonds
- 1/3 cup blueberries or any other berries of your choice
- One pinches salt

Instructions:

1. Take a food processor and make a blend of all these ingredients to make a delicious smoothie.
2. Serve chilled by keeping in the refrigerator.

Keto Fudge Bombs

Cooking Time: 30 minutes

Servings: 12

Ingredients:

- 1 cup soft oil of coconut
- ½ tsp sea salt
- ¼ cup coconut milk, full fat
- ¼ cup sweetener, liquid
- 1 teaspoon vanilla flavor extracts
- ¼ cup cocoa powder, organic
- ½ teaspoon almond flavor extracts

Instructions:

1. Melt the coconut oil and mix oil and milk in a medium bowl. You can use a mixture to complete this work and pour remaining ingredients as well.
2. You need to blend everything to get a smooth blend. Taste the mixture and add sweetener as per your taste.
3. Keep the mold on a baking sheet, line with wax paper and pour almost a tablespoon of batter in each mold. Keep these molds in the freezer with baking sheet and let them settle for 15 minutes.
4. After 15 minutes, pull out with by grabbing the corners of the butter paper. You can cut the fudge

into small squares and then store in the freezer after keeping them secure in an airtight container.

Toffee Flavor Fat Bombs

You can make these healthy bombs with toffee flavors.

Cooking Time: 30 minutes

Servings: 2

Ingredients:

- 1 cup oil, (For your better health, you should choose coconut oil)
- 2 tablespoons butter
- 4 oz cheese, creamy texture
- 3/4 tablespoon cocoa dust
- 1/2 cup of Peanut Butter
- 3 tablespoons flavor of toffee syrup

Instructions:

1. Slowly melt all the ingredients in a small pan because you need a smooth mixture.
2. After melting all the ingredients, you can slowly pour the mixture in the molds and keep in the refrigerator for a few hours.
3. Make them harder and then store in a plastic bag in a freezer for later use.

Salmon Keto Bombs

Get benefits of salmon and lemon sap in this healthy recipe.

Cooking Time: 2 hours

Servings: 12

Ingredients:

- ½ cup cheese cream, full fat
- ⅓ cup butter, pasture
- ½ package grilled salmon
- 1 tablespoon lemon sap
- 1-2 tablespoons dill, chopped
- Salt as per taste

Instructions:

1. In the food processor, you will blend salmon, cheese, and butter. Now add lemon juice and blend again to make the mixture smooth.
2. Place a parchment paper on the tray and pour fat bombs with an even distance on the paper. It will be almost 2 to 2.5 teaspoons for each bomb.
3. Pour dill to garnish and keep in the refrigerator for 1 to 2 hours. You can serve with crunchy leaves of lettuce.

Chapter 6 – Special Ketogenic Fat Bombs

While following a ketogenic diet, you will not get bored because there are lots of interested desserts for you:

Chocolate Chip Bombs

It is a special version of fat bombs with chocolate chip. You can try it during your ketogenic diet.

Cooking Time: 3 hours

Servings: 6

Ingredients

- 2 cups flour, (almond flour is good)
- 2 teaspoons baking soda
- 1 cup coconut, tattered, zero sugar
- 1/2 sweetener
- 1/4 cup protein powder (chocolate flavor)
- 1/4 teaspoon salt
- 4 whole eggs
- 1/4 cup oil, (coconut oil is good)
- 1/4 cup ghee (liquid)
- 1/2 cup whipping cream
- 1 cup blackberries, rinsed
- Sugar-free chocolate chip, 1/3 cups

Toppings:

- Blackberries, 1 cup

- Only 1 sage leaf

Instructions:

1. Grease your slow cooker and pour almond flour, sweetener, protein powder, coconut, baking soda, and salt. Mix them well and keep it aside.
2. Now beat the coconut oil, ghee, eggs and cream for a smooth mixture. Slowly mix berries and chocolate chips in the mixture.
3. Stir in eggs, coconut oil, ghee, and cream, and beat them to make this blend smooth. Gently fold in blackberries and chocolate chips, if using.
4. Pour everything in the slow cooker and set it on a low setting for 3 hours.
5. After three hours, let the slow cooker cook the cake without any heat. You can top the cake with available dressing and keep it on a cooling rack.
6. Make slices to separate bombs as per your requirements.

Keto Fudge Squares

Make delicious fudge squares to serve as Keto bombs. These will be an ideal addition to your diet.

Cooking Time: 2 hours

Servings: 2

Ingredients:

- 3oz chocolate cubes, without sugar
- 1 tablespoons coconut oil
- 1/3 peanut butter
- 2 tablespoons ghee
- 2 tablespoons butter
- 1 tablespoon vanilla syrup (zero sugar)
- 1/3 cup maple syrup (zero sugar)

Instructions:

1. Use a double broiler to melt all the ingredients and mix them all in a pan.
2. Prepare a baking pan with parchment paper and put in the freezer to make them hard.
3. After a few hours, take out of the refrigerator and cut into pieces. You can use for a long time after storing them in a plastic bag.

Chapter 7 - Flavorful Ketogenic Fat Bombs

We have selected some special ketogenic fat bombs with amazing flavors. You must try these bombs with your family.

Mini Tarts with Lemon

Serve these cute tarts without dairy and eggs. These have many nutritional ingredients.

Cooking Time: 45 minutes

Servings: 24

Ingredients:

For Crust:

- 1 pinch salt
- 4 ½ tablespoons melted coconut oil
- 1 ½ teaspoons pure vanilla extract
- 3 tablespoons fresh lemon juice
- 2 tablespoons sugar substitute or as per taste
- 1 cup cashew or almond flour
- ¾ cup dried grated coconut

For Filling:

- 1 pinch salt
- 1 lemon, grated zest
- 2 teaspoons pure lemon extract
- 1 teaspoon vanilla extract, sugar-free

- 3 tablespoons almond or coconut milk
- 1/3 cup lemon juice
- ¼ cup + 1 tablespoon sugar substitute
- ½ cup coconut oil
- *2 tablespoons almond or cashew butter*

Instructions:

1. Grease 2 muffin pans (12-cup size) or small 24 tart pans.
2. Make Crusts: take a bowl and combine all ingredients of crust in this bowl. Mix well. Roll this mixture into small balls and press in your tart pans. Each tart needs almost two teaspoons dough. Chill crust until you are ready to fill it.
3. Make Filling: Put coconut oil and almond or cashew butter in a blender or food processor and whisk well until smooth. Add remaining ingredients of filling and process well to blend. Taste and mix more sweetener or lemon juice as per taste.
4. Pour filling in the crust and chill for almost 30 minutes. Garnish with fresh lemon zest. Serve chilled.

Spicy Cocoa Fat Bombs

These snacks are good to boost the intake of healthy fat.

Cooking Time: 2 hours

Servings: 10

Ingredients:

- 1 cup coconut milk
- 2 tablespoons cocoa powder, unsweetened
- 1 teaspoon vanilla extract, unsweetened
- 1 teaspoon cinnamon
- ¼ teaspoon cayenne pepper
- 2 tablespoons low-car sweetener
- *15 to 20 drops of Stevia extract*

Instructions:

1. Lukewarm coconut milk and put all ingredients in the milk. Mix well to combine all ingredients.
2. Pour this liquid in one ice-cube tray and transfer this tray in freezer for almost 1 to 2 hours. Serve chilled.

Pecan Fudge Bombs

This is a low carb recipe to make delicious fat bombs. Your family will like them.

Cooking Time: 10 minutes

Servings: 10

Ingredients:

- 4 ounces cocoa butter
- ½ cup chopped pecans
- ½ cup melted coconut oil
- 4 talespoons cocoa powder, unsweetened
- 1/3 cup low-fat heavy cream
- 4 tablespoons any Erythritol
- *Silicone molds*

Instructions:

1. Melt coconut oil and cocoa butter together in a double boiler. Beat in cocoa powder to avoid clumps.
2. Pour this blend into your blender. Add erythritol in blender and blender for 2 minutes.
3. Stir in cream and mix for almost 5 minutes to dissolve sugar.
4. Put silicone molds on one sheet pan and fill them halfway with some pecans.
5. Pour the blend of chocolate into desired molds and put in your fridge for almost four hours. Serve chilled.

Flaxseed Fat Bombs

If you love flaxseed meal, you can try these healthy fat bombs.

Preparation time: 1 hour 20 minutes.

Makes 30 servings.

Ingredients:

- Sugar Substitute- 2 cups
- Cocoa powder- ¼ cup
- Milk- ½ cup
- Margarine- ½ cup
- Vanilla extract- 1 teaspoon
- Salt- a pinch
- Low-fat peanut butter- ½ cup
- Flaxseed Meal- 1 cup

Instructions:

1. Take a saucepan and add sugar, cocoa powder, milk and margarine in this pan.
2. Let this mixture boil and mix it well. Turn off heat and let it cool.
3. Stir in the vanilla extract, salt, peanut butter and the flaxseed meal in sugar mixture.
4. Line a tray with waxed paper and use a scoop to drop batter of on waxed paper in round shape.

5. Keep cookies aside for one hour until set. Once the bombs are set, you can store them in an airtight container.

Raisins Fudge Bombs

Get the freshness of raisins and cocoa powder in these bombs.

Preparation time: 16 minutes

Servings: 18

Ingredients:

- Sugar Substitute- 2 cups
- Milk- ½ cup
- Butter- ½ cup
- Peanut butter- ¾ cup
- Chia seeds- 1 1/2 cups
- Cocoa powder- 6 tablespoons
- Vanilla extract- 1 teaspoon
- Raisins- ½ cup

Instructions:

1. In a saucepan, add the sugar substitute, milk and butter and let it boil for at least 1 minute.
2. Remove the saucepan from heat and add in the peanut butter, chia seeds, cocoa powder, vanilla extract and the raisins. Mix well.
3. Drop spoonfuls of the mixture on a tray lined with parchment paper.
4. Put them aside for one hour and serve.
5. Store in airtight containers.

Choco Peanut Fat Bombs

You can make these fat bombs with cocoa powder and peanut butter.

Preparation time: 10 minutes.

30 servings.

Ingredients:

- Milk- ½ cup
- Sugar Substitute- 2 cups
- Cocoa powder- 3 tablespoons
- Crunchy peanut butter- 3 tablespoons
- Butter- ½ cup
- Crushed coconut- 3 cups
- Vanilla extract- 1 teaspoon

Instructions:

1. In a saucepan, add the milk, sugar substitute, cocoa powder, butter and the peanut butter and let them boil over medium heat for 1 1/ 2 minutes and do not stir.
2. Remove the saucepan from heat and let it cool. Now add in the coconut and the vanilla extract.
3. Stir the mixture to make a smooth blend
4. On a waxed paper, drop spoonfuls of the mixture with 1-inch distance.
5. Let them cool before serving. You can store leftover cookies in airtight containers.

Butter and Milk Fat Bombs

Your children will love the taste of these fat bombs.

Preparation time: 15 minutes.

36 servings.

Ingredients:

- Sugar Substitute- 2 cups
- Salt- ½ teaspoon
- Butter- ½ cup
- Milk- ½ cup
- Peanut butter- ½ cup
- Crushed coconut- 3 cups
- Vanilla extract- 1 teaspoon
- Powdered chocolate drink mix- ½ cup

Instructions:

1. Take a saucepan over medium heat and add in the sugar substitute, salt, butter and the milk. Bring the mixture to boil and then boil for 1 minutes.
2. Remove it from heat, cool it and now add in the peanut butter, coconut, vanilla extract and the powdered chocolate drink mix.
3. Drop spoonful of the mixture on a waxed paper.
4. Let the balls rest and cool before serving.

Cereal Fat Bomb

A healthy breakfast for your family members.

Preparation time: 10 minutes.

Makes 36 servings.

Ingredients:

- Brown sugar- ½ cup
- Light corn syrup- 1/3 cup
- Vanilla extract- 1 teaspoon
- Peanut butter- 3/4th cup
- Flake cereal- 3 cups
- Coconut- 1 cup

Instructions:

1. Take a pan and add in the brown sugar and the light corn syrup. Let it boil.
2. When it starts boiling, you can add in the vanilla extract and the peanut butter and stir it well.
3. Remove from heat and add the flake cereal and the coconut.
4. Spray a baking sheet with a nonstick cooking spray and drop spoonful's in the shape of balls on the sheet.
5. Let them cool before serving.

Honey and Chocolate Fat Bombs

Preparation time: 15 minutes.

Serves 16.

Ingredients:

- Thick honey- 1/3 cup
- Chunky peanut butter- ¾ cup
- Vanilla extract- 1 teaspoon
- Almond meal- 1 cup
- Powdered milk- ¾ cup
- Sunflower seeds- ¼ cup
- Chocolate chips- ¼ cups

Instructions:

- In a bowl, add in the thick honey and the peanut butter and mix.
- Now add in the vanilla extract, almond meal and powdered milk. Make sure that all the ingredients are mixed properly.
- Add in the sunflower seeds and mix.
- Shape the mixture in to balls and press to form flat shape or let it be in ball shape.
- Sprinkle with chocolate chips and freeze for 20 minutes before serving.

Christmas Fat Bombs

You can make your Christmas special with these delicious fat bombs.

Preparation time: 20 minutes.

24 servings

Ingredients:

- Milk- 1 cup
- Sugar substitute- 1 cup
- Butter- ¼ cup
- Unsweetened cocoa powder- ¼ cup
- Vanilla extract- 2 teaspoons
- Pumpkin Puree- 1 cup
- Shredded coconut- 2 ½ cups

Instructions:

1. In a pot, add the milk, sugar substitute, butter and cocoa powder. Bring to boil for 3 minutes.
2. Now add in the vanilla extract and bring the mixture to boil for another 2 minutes.
3. Remove from heat and let it cool.
4. Now add in the pumpkin puree and 2 cups of coconut in the milk mixture and mix it well. Cool it.
5. Roll the mixture in to balls. Spread the remaining shredded coconut on a plate and coat the balls in the shredded coconut until properly coated.
6. Set the balls on a piece of parchment paper.

Bourbon no bake cookies

Taste the flavor of bourbon in fat bombs.

Preparation time: 15 minutes.

Makes 12 to 24 cookies.

Ingredients:

- Powdered sugar- 1 cup
- Light karo syrup- 3 tablespoons
- Cocoa powder- 2 1/3 tablespoons
- Crushed vanilla wafers- 3 cups
- Chopped pecans- 1 cup
- Bourbon or rum- ½ cup
- Powdered sugar- to coat

Instructions:

1. With the help of a food processor, crush the pecans and the vanilla wafers until crumbly.
2. Now add in the powdered sugar, light karo syrup, cocoa powder, bourbon and the bourbon and mix all the ingredients.
3. Mix until the ingredients turn smooth.
4. Shape balls from the mixture about 1 inch in diameter.
5. Roll the balls in powdered sugar and chill before serving.

Oleo Fat Bombs

These fat bombs are great for the taste of oleo

Preparation time: 10 minutes.

Makes 24 to 30.

Ingredients:

- Sugar- 2 cups
- Cocoa powder- ½ cup
- Oleo- ¼ lb
- Milk- ½ cup
- Peanut butter- 3 tablespoons
- Vanilla extract- 1 teaspoon
- Shredded coconut- 3 cups

Instructions:

1. In a pan over medium heat add the sugar, cocoa powder, oleo and milk and bring the mixture to a boil.
2. Let it boil for 3 minutes.
3. Remove from heat cool it, add in the peanut butter, vanilla extract and the coconut, and mix well.
4. Drop spoonfuls on waxed paper and let them set before serving.

Chocolate Butter Fat Bombs

I personally love this recipe because of chocolate chips and soft butter.

Preparation time: 35 minutes.

Makes 35 servings.

Ingredients:

- Soft butter- 1 cup
- Packed brown sugar- 1 ½ cups
- Vanilla extract- 2 teaspoons
- Salt- ½ teaspoon
- All purpose flour- 2 cups
- Water- 1 tablespoon
- Mini chocolate chips- 6 ounce

Instructions:

1. Beat the butter and the brown sugar until smooth and creamy.
2. Add in the vanilla extract, salt, flour, water and the chocolate chips.
3. Mix everything well.
4. Make balls from the mixture and freeze them.
5. Let them come at room temperature before serving.

Flaked Coconut Fat Bombs

Coconut lovers must try this unique taste.

Preparation time: 50 minutes

36 servings

Ingredients:

- Semi-sweet chocolate chips- 1 cup
- Butter- 1/3 cup
- Large marshmallows- 16
- Creamy peanut butter- 1/3 cup
- Vanilla extract- ½ teaspoon
- Flaked coconut- 1 cup
- Almond meal- 2 cups

Instructions:

1. Set a double boiler on a stove and melt the chocolate chips, butter and the marshmallows.
2. Mix until smooth and remove from heat.
3. Now add the peanut butter, vanilla extract, flaked coconut and the almond meal and mix everything properly.
4. Drop spoonfuls on a waxed paper and refrigerate for about 30 minutes or until they are set.
    5. *Serve!*

Pudding Fat Bombs

Taste of vanilla and chocolate pudding will give a unique flavor to these bombs.

Preparation time: 25 minutes

Makes 48 servings.

Ingredients:

- Sugar substitute- 2 cups
- Butter- ¾ cup
- Milk- 2/3 cup
- Instant chocolate pudding mix- 3.9 ounce
- Coconut flakes- 3 ½ cups
- Vanilla extract- ½ teaspoon

Instructions:

1. Take a pan, add in the sugar, butter and milk, and bring it to boil. Boil for 2 minutes.
2. Turn off the heat and cool slightly.
3. Add the chocolate pudding mix, coconut flakes and the vanilla extract.
4. Mix everything well and then drop spoonfuls on a waxed paper.
5. *Serve!*

Applesauce Fat Bombs

You can do something different with fat bombs by adding applesauce.

Preparation time: 35 minutes

Makes 40 servings

Ingredients:

- Sugar substitute- 1 2/3 cups
- Milk- ½ cup
- Cocoa powder- ½ cup
- Salt- 1/8 teaspoon
- Peanut butter- ½ cup
- Applesauce- 5 tablespoons
- Vanilla extract- 1 teaspoon
- Crushed apple- 3 cups

Instructions:

1. In a saucepan add the sugar, milk and cocoa powder, bring it to a boil, and cook for 1 minute.
2. Remove the saucepan from heat and cool it slightly.
3. Now add the peanut butter, applesauce, salt and the vanilla extract and mix until completely smooth.
4. Now mix in the apples.
5. Drop spoonfuls on a waxed paper and cool them completely before removing.
6. **Serve!**

Hazelnut Fat Bombs

If you like nutty flavor, this recipe is only for you.

Preparation time: 20 minutes

Makes 72 servings.

Ingredients:

- Granulated sugar- 2 cups
- Cocoa powder- 6 tablespoons
- Vegetable oil- ½ cup
- Milk- ½ cup
- Crushed Coconut- 3 cups
- Chopped hazelnuts- 1 cup
- Chocolate hazelnut spread- 2/3 cup
- Vanilla extract- 1 teaspoon

Instructions:

1. Take a saucepan and add in the sugar, cocoa powder, chocolate hazelnut spread and the milk.
2. Cook until the mixture comes to boil.
3. Boil until 1 minute and continue to stir it.
4. Remove the pan from heat and cool it.
5. Now add in the vegetable oil, coconut, chopped hazelnuts and the vanilla extract.
6. Mix properly the entire ingredients.
7. Line cookie sheets with waxed paper.
8. Drop spoonsful from the mixture and keep them in the fridge.

9. You can even store them in airtight containers.

Date Fat Bombs

Dates are healthy for everyone. You will like the taste of these bombs.

Preparation time: 1 hour 30 minutes

Makes about 12 cookies

Ingredients:

- Pecan halves- 1 cup
- Shredded unsweetened coconut- ½ cup
- Soft mejdool dates, preferably pitted, - 10 to 11
- Coconut oil- 1 tablespoons
- Sea salt- ½ teaspoon
- Vanilla extract- ½ teaspoon
- Arrow root or tapioca starch- ½ cup
- Extra arrow root or tapioca starch- for filling

Directions:

1. Take a baking sheet, line it with a parchment paper, and then set it aside.
2. Take a food processor, add in inside the pecan halves and the shredded unsweetened coconut, and blend until the pecans and coconut are finely ground.
3. Now add in the soft dates, the coconut oil and blend.
4. Further add in the sea salt, vanilla extract and blend.
5. Finally add in the arrow root or the tapioca starch and process until it forms a sticky dough. If the

dough stick together between your fingers, it is ready.
6. Make fat bombs with this dough and put in the fridge to serve chilled.

Marshmallow Fat Bombs

Raisins and marshmallow can do wonder in fat bombs.

Preparation time: 10 minutes

Makes 36 servings

Ingredients:

- Semi-sweet chocolate chips- 1 cup
- Light butter- 5 tablespoons
- Large marshmallows-14
- Vanilla extract- 1 teaspoon
- Shredded raisins or any combination of dry fruit mix, shredded coconut, miniature marshmallows or chopped nuts- 2/3 cup
- Almond meal- 2 cups

Instructions:

1. Take a saucepan and add the semi-sweet chocolate chips, butter and the large marshmallows.
2. Heat them on low heat and stir, until it turns to a smooth mixture.
3. Remove the saucepan from heat.
4. Cool slightly.
5. Now add in the vanilla extract.
6. Now add the almond meal, and the shredded raisins, dry fruit mix, or shredded coconut (depends on your choice).
7. Mix properly so that all the ingredients are incorporated well.

8. Drop spoonfuls in round shape on the waxed paper, cover them, and keep in the fridge for almost 2 to 3 hours.
9. Let them come at room temperature before serving.

Samoa Fudge Keto Bombs

These lovely bombs are free from grain so great for your ketogenic diet.

Cooking Time: 2 hours

Servings: 10

Ingredients:

Fudge Ingredients:

- 3 ½ tablespoon cocoa powder, unsweetened
- 2 ½ tablespoons melted butter
- 2 ½ tablespoons melted coconut oil
- 3 ½ tablespoons sweetener or coconut sugar
- *2 tablespoons coconut milk, unsweetened*

Caramel Ingredients:

- 2 ½ tablespoons sweetener
- 2 ½ tablespoons butter
- 2 tablespoons coconut milk
- 1/8 teaspoon molasses or maple syrup, low carb
- *1/8 teaspoon vanilla extract*

For Garnishing:

- *1 tablespoon shredded coconut, unsweetened*

Instructions:

1. Combine all ingredients of fudge bomb in a bowl and mix well. Pour this blend into a greased ice cube tray or candy mold.
2. Freeze for almost 30 minutes.
3. Put a small pan over medium flame and melt butter (2 ½ tablespoons) for caramel coating.
4. Add sweetener (2 ½ tablespoons) in melted butter, coconut milk (2 tablespoons) and molasses (1/8 teaspoon). Stir and cook until bubbling. Turn off the stove and mix in vanilla extract (1/8 teaspoon). Leave caramel sauce for a few minutes to make it thick.
5. Remove fat bombs from your freezer and put on one baking sheet (lined with wax paper).
6. Drizzle caramel sauce over bombs. Sprinkle with some shredded coconut.
7. Serve or store in an airtight jar. Put this jar in your freezer.

Conclusion

Ketogenic fat bombs contain healthy fat, so it is alright to include them in your ketogenic diet. The recipes of bombs use the sugar substitute like stevia that is a zero-carb and low-calorie sweetener. It can't cause any stomach problem just like sugar alcohols. These bombs are especially crucial in the ketogenic diet because healthy fats are essential to decrease inflammation in the body.

You must store these fat bombs in your fridge in airtight containers. You can keep them for 1 to 2 weeks. If you have kept them in your freezer, make sure to thaw them before serving. Try 50 delicious ketogenic fat bombs recipes of this book and make your every day special.

Part 2

INTRODUCTION

Our daily routine consists of a variety of meals including main courses, snacks, desserts, etc. There is so much on the menu that we can forget the importance of certain foods and the role they can play in improving our physical health. Fat bombs play a vital role in improving our physical health.

In this book, you'll learn more about the ingredients you can use, as well as some great recipes you can follow. We will provide you with a delicious dish for the different types of Fat bombs you can have: sweet, savoury and frozen

This book was perhaps my most challenging and creative challenge to date. So I hope you take advantage of these Fat bombs and they will help you stay in keto by adding a little variety and fun to your diet.

What Is Ketogenic Diet ?

What is a keto diet? A keto diet is a low carb diet that forces the body to produce ketones for use as a source of energy. Ketones are produced in the liver from fatty acids. The ketogenic diet is also called keto diet, low carb diet, LCHF (low carb), ketosis diet. There are other forms derived from the keto diet, such as the carnivorous diet, the carbohydrate-free diet, the keto-cyclic diet and the targeted ketone diet.

In recent years, we have seen how the landscape of health and well-being has changed. People have become more aware of the food they put in their bodies. Whatever the reason why people choose different diets and dietary options, health has always been the main concern.

In recent years, we have become familiar with diets like Atkins, Paleo and the South Beach Diet. We even saw celebrities promote these diets! Now, the keto diet is the new kid on the block. It's fashionable, but does it resist all the hype ?!

The ketogenic diet is another diet that is gaining popularity in recent years. So what is the ketogenic diet? What makes it different from other diets? Here are some important things you need to know if you plan or know someone who follows this diet.

What is ketosis?

In a ketogenic diet, the term "ketosis" refers to the metabolic state whereby the body turns into fatty acids and ketone bodies as the main substrate of the fuel, especially for the heart, the skeletal muscles. It was traditionally the mechanism used by humans and other animals to survive during times of famine. However, today it is possible to deliberately induce nutritional ketosis by severely restricting carbohydrates and moderately moderating proteins.

What is nutritional ketosis?

Nutritional ketosis occurs when your body uses fatty acids and ketones as the main source of fuel instead of glucose. This occurs when carbohydrates are restricted and ketone bodies are produced in the liver.

Acetoacetate (AcAc) and D-β-hydroxybutyrate (βHB) ketone bodies are two of the three ketone bodies produced and serve as an alternative fuel source. The metabolic actions of ketone bodies are based on strong evolutionary principles to prolong survival in the event of caloric deprivation.

Before ketogenic diets were used to treat epilepsy, ketones were normally present only during famine. Today, keto diets are used not only to treat epilepsy, but also for diabetes, Parkinson's disease, dementia, autism, depression, weight loss, physical performance and much more. !

What is ketogenesis?

Ketogenesis is the production of ketone bodies. Ketones are insulin-independent, water-soluble, fat-derived fuels that can be used by the brain. This adaptation is associated with a small loss of ketoacids in the urine (100-150 mM / day or 40-60 calories / day). Therefore, when you start a keto diet, you will check for ketones in your urine.

What are endogenous ketones?

The ketone bodies produced in the liver are more specifically called endogenous ketone bodies.

What are exogenous ketones?

Exogenous ketone bodies are only ketone bodies ingested via a nutritional supplement. They are made outside the body. Technically, you can follow a high carbohydrate diet, ingest exogenous ketones, and then be in a state of ketosis within about 30 minutes.

Most supplements use BHB as the source of their exogenous ketone bodies. BHB is converted to acetoacetic acid and then converted into acetone through an acetoacetate decarboxylase process, acetone will be excreted. Part of the acetoacetic acid will enter the energy pathway using beta-ketothialase, which converts acetoacetic acid into two molecules of Acetyl-CoA.

Acetyl-CoA is then able to enter the Krebs cycle and generate ATP. Exogenous ketone supplements provide users with an instant supply of ketones. Even if you are not in a state of ketosis before ingestion (for example, if you follow a diet rich in carbohydrates).

What is a keto diet?

The classic ketogenic diet is a high-fat diet developed in the 1920s to mimic the biochemical changes associated with periods of food shortage. The diet consists of 80 to 90% fat, with carbohydrates and proteins making up the rest of the intake.

The diet provides enough protein for growth, but insufficient amounts of carbohydrate for the metabolic needs of the body. The energy comes largely from the use of body fat and the fat provided in the diet. These fats are converted into beta-hydroxybutyrate, acetoacetate and acetone, ketone bodies that represent an alternative source of energy to glucose.

How does the body make ketones?

Most animal cells can make cholesterol, but cholesterol is mainly made in the liver. Short and medium chain saturated fats are converted to ketones in the liver and some of these ketones are used to make cholesterol. Ketones (not glucose) are also the preferred energy source for virtually all cells in the body, including the brain.

Much of a healthy human body consists of fats and cholesterol. Nearly half of cell walls (cell membranes) consist of cholesterol; saturated fats are another major component of all cells.

What are the ketogenic diets used at the moment?

The ketogenic diet is well established as a treatment for persistent epilepsy. This treatment should be considered as a first-line treatment for type 1 glucose transporter and pyruvate dehydrogenase deficiency. It should be considered early in the treatment of Dravet syndrome and myoclonic-astatic epilepsy (Doose syndrome).

Early studies indicate that the ketogenic diet appears to be effective in other metabolic conditions, including phosphofructokinase deficiency and glycogenosis type V (McArdle's disease).

More and more publications suggest that the ketogenic diet may be beneficial in certain neurodegenerative diseases, including Alzheimer's disease, Parkinson's disease and amyotrophic lateral sclerosis. In these disorders, the ketogenic diet appears to be neuroprotective, promoting improved mitochondrial function and saving the production of adenosine triphosphate.

Do ketogenic diets have therapeutic properties?

Dietary therapy is a promising intervention for cancer, as it can target the relative ineffectiveness of tumors in using ketone bodies as an alternative source of fuel. The ketogenic diet may also play a role in improving outcomes of trauma and hypoxic injury.

What are the signs that you are in ketosis?

Positive blood ketones

Positive urinary ketones if you are a beginner (this means that you produce ketones, but you do not use them as fuel because they are excreted)

Increased urination, a keto diet initially acts as a diuretic since you eliminate carbohydrates that retain water

A fruity odor breathes (this comes from the production of acetone)

Decreased appetite

Increased energy

Improved mood

Is a Keto diet dangerous?

Ketosis simply means that your body produces ketone bodies. You burn fat instead of glucose. Ketosis is not necessarily harmful to health.

Ketosis itself is not particularly dangerous, it's something to watch for, especially if you have type 1 diabetes. Ketosis can be a precursor to ketoacidosis, also known as diabetic ketoacidosis.

Ketoacidosis is a condition characterized by high levels of glucose and ketone. Ketoacidosis makes the blood too acidic. It is more common in people with type 1 than type 2 diabetes. Once the symptoms of ketoacidosis start, they can escalate very quickly.

The symptoms of ketoacidosis include:

A breath that smells like fruity or nail polish or nail polish remover

Fast breathing or shortness of breath

Excessive thirst

Frequent urination

Stomach pain

Nausea vomiting

Fatigue, weakness

Confusion

Coma

Are there any negative side effects of a ketogenic diet?

Like any other diet, the ketogenic diet can have side effects because your body adapts to a new way of eating. Short-term effects are obvious when you start the diet with your fist.

hypoglycemia

Excessive thirst

Frequent urination

Tired

Hunger

Confusion, anxiety and / or irritability

tachycardia

Dizziness and tremors

Sweating and chills

However, there are long-term effects for people who have been following a ketogenic diet for some time. Since the therapy has been over-used in children with epilepsy and seizures, kidney stones, also known as nephrolithiasis, are a common complication in children following the diet. About 5% of patients suffer from it.

It is however treatable and current recommendations suggest that the diet should be continued.

In addition, patients have an increased risk of bone fractures. This stems from changes in insulin-like growth factor 1 levels and the effects of acidosis. Acidosis causes bone erosion, weakens bones and makes them vulnerable to fractures.

In order to manage these side effects, vitamin and mineral supplements are routinely administered to patients following the ketogenic diet. This usually includes a multivitamin, calcium and vitamin D supplements.

For adults on a ketogenic diet, the most common complications are weight loss, constipation and increased cholesterol levels. Women may also experience amenorrhea or other disturbances of the menstrual cycle.

What future for ketogenic diets?

Although several studies have been conducted to validate the efficacy of the ketogenic diet, questions about the diet remain unanswered by practitioners. Since the ketogenic diet has been used for decades to control seizures in children with epilepsy, issues such as the duration and duration of the plan to confer long-term benefit are still uncertain.

The future is bright for weight loss and diabetes. Virta Health has just published a research article reporting on its one-year study of patients with type 2 diabetes. The results were amazing!

Quick overview of the study:

349 adults with T2D enrolled:

218 participants (83%) remained enrolled at 1 year.

HbA1c decreased from 59.6 ± 1.0 to 45.2 ± 0.8 mmol mol-1

Weight down 13.8 ± 0.71 kg

The prescription of drugs for T2DM other than metformin decreased from $56.9 \pm 3.1\%$ to $29.7 \pm 3.0\%$

Insulin therapy was reduced or eliminated in 94% of users !!!

The sulfonylureas have been completely eliminated.

No adverse events were attributed to the Continuing Care Intervention Group.

HsCRP - 39%

Triglycerides - 24%

HDL-cholesterol + 18%

Serum creatinine and liver enzymes (ALT, AST and ALP) decreased

Participants in the usual care group (education provided by physicians and the diabetes education program) had no significant change in biomarkers or medication prescription for T2D at one year.

This shows that a ketogenic diet can COMPLETELY the standard of care, namely diabetes education programs offered by licensed diabetes educators and other diabetes educators. This is just one of many articles published on the potential benefits of a ketogenic diet.

What Are The Benefits Of A Ketogenic Diet?

The ketogenic diet is a diet low in carbohydrates and high in protein. When you understand the role of fats in a healthy metabolism, you understand why the ketogenic diet offers so many benefits when it is well done.

Fats are used in everything, and I'm talking about all the metabolic processes. Every cell in your body is a small fat bubble - phospholipidic membrane. Even muscle cells, blood cells, bone cells, but especially skin cells and nerve cells. Every cell!

Having said that, have a brief overview of the top ten benefits of the ketogenic diet:

Higher Energy Levels - Dawn Til 'Dusk

Most people notice an increase in their energy level after about a week of keto consumption. Sometimes it can take a little longer and at other times it only takes a few days or two.

But believe me, when that happens, it's very noticeable. No more sugar ups and downs in the afternoon. You can expect a constant flow of energy throughout the day.

In addition to that, you can expect higher levels of concentration, less brain fog (even if you did not know it), deeper, more satisfying sleep, and a more restful and crisper awakening. go.

Improved sleep quality

I talked about it briefly in the last point because the two are related and here's why. The ketogenic diet helps regulate your hormones. Did I mention that most hormones are made from fat? Yes, it's true. They are called Eicosanoids and you can see on their entry in the wiki that they are involved in just about everything. It is through their study that we have discovered essential fatty acids - they are essential because they need them to make eicosanoids!

Because these local hormones affect the creation of other hormones, they help regulate everything from body temperature to hunger, weight, growth and of course the woman's monthly cycle and of course the process of menopause. Again, there is virtually no metabolic process that does not use a lot of hormones.

Healthy and safe weight loss

The ketogenic diet does not require you to starve yourself in any way. In fact, we encourage you to eat as much food as you can. The idea behind this is not to limit your fat intake in particular. They help you stay full longer and you have to train your body to burn fat for fuel instead of glucose.

We all have the ability to do this, but after a "traditional" Western diet for years and sometimes decades, our body no longer uses its fat-burning ability. This is why, although your body produces ketones and contracts ketosis in a few days, it may take longer to become fully keto-adapted.

Once you are keto-ready, you can expect all the excess fat that you have won just to start melting while still feeding you a lot of healthy fat, vegetables, and protein.

Delicious food

Do you know all the "low fat" foods in the supermarket that claim to be healthy? Well, they have a terrible taste ... or at least they would if the food manufacturers had not accumulated a ton of sugar to hide the fact that they were bland and tasteless.

You know why they are bland and tasteless?

That's because fat is what makes things delicious! Not only that, the fat is so satiating. You will end up eating much smaller portions, but as long as you maintain your fat intake you will find that you are not as hungry all day long. You will also find that you can stay several hours without eating, without feeling bad, without turning your head or if you do not feel "stuffy"

My meals consist of my favorite green vegetables, delicious meat like pork belly or chicken legs (with skin), topped with homemade mayonnaise and some generous spoonfuls of grass-fed butter. So good. Most of the recipes I still use to date come from the Keto meal plans I started with.

Hormonal balance / healing

The high carbohydrate and fat diet that most of us have to follow is catastrophic for your hormonal health.

In fact, recommendations for a healthy diet in the West, recommending a diet low in fat and high in carbohydrates, were introduced almost at the same time as levels of obesity and heart disease and that diabetes began to increase. Coincidence? I do not think so.

The ketogenic diet, in its initial phase, is to rebalance and heal your hormonal systems. The sudden presence of an excess of good fats and a shortage of carbohydrates and sugars triggers the natural healing process of your body. You've all heard how your controlled fasting can be beneficial, and when you fast, your body goes into ketosis.

We all have between 40 and 60,000 calories stored in our bodies, and the reason a healthy person can stay for about three weeks without eating anything is because the body switches to ketosis and uses these reserves.

This means that when you trigger a ketosis with the ketogenic diet, you trigger healing and induce your body's natural ability to burn fat. The net result - more sustained energy levels, your body still having access to its reserves.

An end to the desires

We have all had them. If you're a bit like me, you know that cravings can be the bane of your existence. You feel that you need this cookie or cake more than anything you need. Then you eat it, you feel good during the time it takes, and soon after you receive a drop of sugar, and you must either eat more, or you will become really crazy, or you will be depressed , or sleepy, or all three!

The Keto Diet is the ultimate way to say goodbye to these cravings for good. You will get rid of your sugar and carbohydrate addiction and, instead, provide your body with high quality nutrients, and it will love you for that.

The end of health problems

The advantages of the Keto diet are roughly doubles. By reducing the stress your carbohydrate puts on your system, you're improving a host of related issues. Plus, by increasing the availability of good fats in your system, you provide your body with high quality fuel and the basics for healing.

Take Eczema, Asthma, Acne and PMS.

These complaints often go together because they are all dysfunctions of the inflammatory and immune system. The inflammatory system is obviously helpful when your body needs to fight an infection or heal itself. Likewise, the immune system is what keeps us healthy.

Good fats are the building blocks of systems that regulate immunity and inflammation. It's still those good old eicosanoids. Of course, eicosanoids are also used in the process of uterine contraction. So you may find that not having enough can give you menstrual pain, hormonal blemishes, seasonal allergies and make your eczema and asthma ten times worse than it should be.

Eicosanoids also help regulate the mood control system and sleep triggers.

Regulation of the menstrual cycle

All these systems are linked, so you will find that improving a system tends to improve many things. The key here is hormonal balance and healing, which your body naturally begins to do as soon as you enter the keto lifestyle.

Regulation of mood

Once again, this is a fallout from this double imperative of reducing your carbohydrates and increasing your consumption of healthy fats.

Your premenstrual syndrome disappears, your spots disappear, your skin shines, your hair shines, your eyes are bright because you sleep well. You have so much energy that you can really start putting yourself in life.

How is your mood? Even without the increased levels of hormonal health and mood regulators in your system, when you're feeling healthy, your mood is good, is not it?

Here, it's not really rocket science!

Allergy Relief

An allergic reaction is essentially a high alert state of your system to foreign bodies coming in contact with your membranes. It has been shown that high carbohydrate diets can over-stimulate the production of cortisol in the system, which can lead to a higher prevalence of allergic reactions.

Cutting carbohydrates and increasing fat in a ketogenic way can again solve this problem on both sides: you stop over-stimulating inflammation and depressing the immune system, and you start giving the two systems more basic material that it can needs to function efficiently and effectively.

The body is a holistic system - what I mean is that all parts are designed to work together.

What are Fat Bombs?

"Fat Bombs" looks disgusting. I imagine a small round ball of deflating fat that explodes when I hear its name. But I finally got over it and fell in love! You know my sweet tooth. Well, the big bombs satisfy him while allowing me to stay healthy. It's not better than that!

What are Fat Bombs?

Fat bombs are homemade pieces made from a mix of foods high in fats and carbohydrates. Coconut oil, coconut cream, coconut butter, nuts, butter and cream cheese are among the high-fat foods, although any healthy fat can be used. It still does not sound so good, huh? Well, read on!

Healthy fats are important for many reasons, and fat bombs have become a way for people on a low carb or ketogenic diet to add calories to their daily diet without adding carbohydrates to the menu. Let me explain.

A diet low in carbohydrates but high in fat causes a state of ketosis in the body. This is a natural state in which the body lacks simple sugars and so begins to burn stored fat instead of carbohydrates. The ketogenic diet became popular in the 1920s as part of the treatment of epilepsy. Although it is still used for this, and also as a natural cancer treatment, it has become increasingly popular in recent years with bodybuilders and those who need to lose weight.

I use them to satisfy my sweet tooth, but also so that my family gets all the healthy fat we need to stay in shape. As the brain and body of my children continue to grow, they need a lot of healthy fat in their diet and fat bombs are an easy way to get them to eat it. They think it's candy, right? ?? Fat bombs also provide protein, fiber and energy boost without high sugar.

How to make fat bombs

Large bombs usually contain at least 85% fat. Making them is easy. You basically need to:

Your fatty base (coconut oil, butter and cream, cream cheese, butter, for example)

Low carbohydrate flavors or sweeteners (eg, cocoa powder, flavored stevia, spices)

Other healthy additions with low carbohydrate content (seeds, nuts, dried fruits, coconuts)

What Are The Benefits Of Fat Bombs?

I like to use coconut oil in fat bombs because it has many health benefits:

Reduces the risk of heart disease

Reduces the risk of hypertension

Reduces inflammation and arthritis

Protects against cancer

Strengthens the immune system (anti-bacterial, anti-fungal, anti-viral)

Increases brain function and memory

Prevents osteoporosis

Improves skin irritations

Improve type II diabetes

Slows down the signs of aging

Improves liver and gallbladder function

Helps balance hormones

Improves digestion

Increases energy and stamina

Build muscle

For those of you who are focused on weight loss, coconut oil is wonderful to add to your diet:

Helps your body burn fat

Is used immediately for energy, rather than being stored

Decreases appetite

Helps to get rid of belly fat, especially

Why should you eat fat bombs

Even though we have been told for more than 20 years to reduce fat, scientists are finally proving that a healthy fat is needed. Eating fat bombs adds healthy fat to your diet in a delicious way. It is not necessary to eat a handful of coconut oil every morning to get the most out of it, just throw some big bombs!

Healthy fats provide important nutrients to the heart, skin, lungs, brain and immune system. And if you thought ketosis was just weight loss, think again! Stay in a healthy ketosis state:

Reduces the risk of heart disease

Decreases insulin sensitivity

Reduces the risk of developing type II diabetes

Lowers triglycerides

Decreases belly fat

Reduces the severity of acne

Lowers blood pressure

Decreases the symptoms of Parkinson's disease

Reduces total cholesterol and HDL "bad" cholesterol

Reduces the risk of Alzheimer's disease

"Dying" cancer cells

So you can feel good about adding fat bombs to your diet, no matter how disgusting the name sounds. Believe me, once you've tried one, you will not be afraid of their name!

Essential Fat Bomb Ingredients

Here are some of the essential ingredients for making fat bombs:

Nuts

Seeds

Coconut

Coconut oil

Cocoa butter

Fat dairy products

Activated nuts and seeds

Activated nuts and seeds (think of soaking or sprouting) are preferable because they are easier to digest and their nutrients are better absorbed. Roasting also helps reduce levels of phytic acid, which inhibits the absorption of nutrients during digestion, but soaking nuts is more effective. In addition, soaking and drying produce a crispier texture and a more delicious flavor.

Soaking nuts is simple. Place them in a bowl filled with water or salt water and leave them at room temperature overnight. Drain and spread on baking sheet lined with parchment paper and place in oven or dehydrator for 12 to 24 hours, turning occasionally until completely dry. . See the box on the next page for dewatering temperatures. keep in a tightly closed Container

Coconut Products

The desiccated coconut is a shredded and dehydrated coconut meat. Always use the unsweetened variety.

Coconut flour is a finely ground coconut flour from which the oil has been removed.

Coconut butter is made from dehydrated coconut meat in the same way as nut and seed butters.

Coconut milk is the liquid extracted from the grated meat of a coconut. You can also find it in its dehydrated form in the form of coconut milk powder.

Coconut milk cream or coconut cream is the fat part of the coconut milk separated from the aqueous part. If a recipe calls for creamed coconut milk, do it one day in advance. To "cream" the coconut milk, simply place the box in the refrigerator overnight. The next day, open the tin can, pour the coconut milk solidified with a spoon and discard the liquids. Do not shake the box before opening it. A 14-ounce can (400 g) will yield about 7 ounces (200 g) of coconut cream.

Coconut oil is the fat extracted from ripe coconut meat. It is rich in saturated fatty acids and medium chain triglycerides (MCT) that are easy to digest. Remember that coconut oil melts at room temperature and all treats prepared from it must be refrigerated.

Cacao and Chocolate

Cocoa butter or cocoa butter is a pure fat extracted from cocoa beans. It has a high smoke point and a long life. It consists mainly of saturated and monounsaturated fatty acids. Unlike coconut oil, it stays solid at room temperature.

Cocoa paste - also called cocoa liquor or unsweetened chocolate - is a pure cocoa mass and becomes liquid when heated. It contains both cocoa solids and cocoa butter.

Cocoa powder is often called cocoa, but technically, raw cocoa powder is made from raw cocoa mass, while cocoa powder is made from roasted cocoa and may also contain oils, fats and oils. , milk or sugar added. Make sure to choose a version without sugar!

Cocoa beans are cocoa beans that have been simmered, isolated from their husks and reduced to pieces. They are sometimes confused with dull chocolate chips - as different as a dark chocolate, the bursts of cocoa do not contain sugar.

Dark chocolate or sweet and sour chocolate is made with a minimum of 70% cocoa solids. Personally, I never use chocolate containing less than 85 to 90% cocoa. The more cocoa there is, the less sugar it contains, which means it causes less cravings!

Sweet Fat Bomb Recipes

Coconut Berry Delights

ingredients

1 cup of refined coconut oil

1/2 cup mixed frozen fruits such as raspberries, blueberries, pomegranates, cherries and strawberries

1 teaspoon of vanilla extract

14 drops SweetLeaf Clear Liquid Stevia (or substitute honey to taste)

Instructions

Melt the coconut oil gently on the stove. While the oil is melting, briefly process the frozen fruit in a food processor to chop it into small pieces. (If you are concerned that your berries are excessively cold, refer to the note above in the "Recipe Notes" section.)

Add vanilla extract and stevia to your food processor.

Pour the melted coconut oil into your food processor and mix with the fruits and other ingredients. Continue mixing until all the fruits are well mixed with the oil.

The mixture should now be a thick mixed consistency. If, for any reason, your mixture is still frozen and mixed, you can remove some of the frozen pieces and melt them gently on your stove. Once melted, put the mixture back into your food processor and try mixing it again.

Pour the finished mixture into molds or simply place spoonfuls on a surface lined with parchment paper, such as a cutting board. Using the mussels will make your coconut delights more beautiful, but simply dropping them with a spoon is just as good if you do not have or want to use mussels.

Put mussels or a parchment-lined surface in the freezer to enhance the pleasures. After about half an hour, or each time they become solid, remove the mussels / parchment paper and store in a freezer. Enjoy whenever you feel you need (or desire!) Coconut oil.

Fudge Fat Bombs

ingredients:

1 cup of SunButter Almond Butter or Sunflower Butter without nuts and no added sugar

1 cup coconut oil, at room temperature

1/2 cup of unsweetened cocoa powder

1/3 cup of coconut flour

1/4 c. In powdered stevia OR 1 to 2 tbsp. Sweetener with monk fruit, according to the preferred taste.

1/16 c. Teas of pink Himalayan salt

Optional material:

Silicone mold

Instructions:

Over medium heat in a small saucepan, melt and mix almond butter and coconut oil. In the same jar, add the dry ingredients and stir until well blended.

Allow the mixture to cool slightly and test the taste to determine if an additional sweetener is needed. Add more if necessary according to your preferences.

Pour the mixture into the bowl and transfer it to the freezer so that it solidifies, about 60 to 90 minutes, depending on the temperature of your freezer OR in a silicone mold (if you choose to use a mold in silicone, skip Steps 4 and 5 and just let the big bombs to solidify in the freezer, about 2-3 hours).

Once solidified, remove the bowl from the freezer and form balls. Tip: Wash your hands regularly with cold water and wipe with a dry paper towel to prevent the coconut oil from melting into your hands. Place the formed balls on a tray or plate and return to the freezer for 15 to 20 minutes. Enjoy!

Chocolate Peanut Butter Fat Bombs

Ingredients

Chocolate layer:

2 Tablespoon of melted coconut oil

4 tablespoons peanut butter

4 tablespoons Unsweetened cocoa powder

1/4 Tablespoon of vanilla extract

1/4 tsp Liquid stevia (I used 1/4 cup Swerve confectioners instead)

Layer of peanut butter:

2 Tablespoons of melted coconut oil

4 Tablespoons Peanut butter or almond

1/4 Tablespoon of vanilla extract

1/4 tsp Liquid stevia (I used 1/4 cup Swerve confectioners instead)

Instructions

Chocolate layer

1) Combine all the ingredients for the chocolate layer, mix until smooth.

2) Pour the muffin cups and freeze them for about 10 minutes.

Layer of peanut butter

1) Combine all the ingredients for the peanut butter layer.

2) Pour over the chocolate.

3) Freeze until firm.

4) Keep refrigerated or frozen until eating

Caramel Apple Pie Fat Bomb Recipe

Ingredients:

- 2 medium green organic apples, seeded and sliced (if you want to peel them, it's up to you, it's not me)

- 2 Tablespoon of coconut oil

- 1 teaspoon of cinnamon

- 1 can of coconut cream

- 1/2 cup of coconut butter

- 20 drops english toffee stevia

- pinch of sea salt

Instructions:

- In a frying pan, sauté the apples in the coconut oil until they are tender

- Add the cinnamon and stir to coat well

- In a powerful mixer, mix the remaining ingredients and mix at maximum power until liquefied

- Pour into silicone molds (go ahead, give it a taste! The "dough" is so tasty!)

- Place in the freezer until firm

- Pop out of molds and store them in a plastic bag in the refrigerator

key lime pie fat bombs

ingredients:

2 cups raw cashews, boiled 12 minutes or soaked 2 hours

1 cup of coconut oil, melted

1/2 cup of coconut butter

3/4 cup lime juice

1/8 tsp - 1/4 tspPowdered stevia (depending on your sweetness preferences)

Materials :

Food processor

Instructions :

- Combine all ingredients in the food processor and mix until well blended.

- Transfer the mixture to a medium sized bowl and place in the freezer for 20-30 minutes to allow it to cool (they may take a little longer to cool if you choose to boil the cashews rather than soaking them).

- Remove the mixture from the freezer and form balls.

- Place the balls in the freezer for 20 minutes to harden. I recommend putting them on a cookie sheet or parchment-lined plate to prevent the bottom from sticking.

- Remove from the freezer once solid. Store them in an airtight container in the refrigerator or freezer (you should let them defrost a little before eating if you choose to freeze them).

Keto Easter Egg Cookie Dough Fat Bombs

ingredients:

2 cups (235 grams) Bob's Red Mill almond flour

½ cup (100 grams) of coconut oil, melted

1 teaspoon (5 ml) vanilla extract without alcohol

5-10 drops of non-alcoholic stevia

¼ teaspoon (1 gram) of gray sea salt

Cup (70 g) of dark chocolate without sugar coating

½ cup (112 grams) of melted coconut butter

Easter-themed natural food coloring

Instructions:

- Spread parchment paper or silicone baking mat on a large baking sheet.

- Add almond flour, coconut oil, vanilla, stevia and salt to your food processor using an "S" blade. Treat until smooth, about 20 seconds.

- Add the chocolate chips. Collect about 1.5 tablespoon and roll into a ball between your palms. Place on a prepared baking sheet and flatten to form a large egg. Continue with the rest of the dough.

- Transfer the plate to the freezer and let cool for 1 hour.

- Place a cooling rack on a second baking tray and set aside.

- Prepare the icing by melting the coconut butter, dividing it into several dishes and adding food coloring.

- Remove the Keto cookie dough eggs from the freezer. Dip only 1 side of each into the coconut butter and place the prepared medium. Add the rest of the colored coconut butter in a Ziploc bag, cut out the tip and pour on it.

- Transfer the eggs to the cooling rack in the refrigerator for 1 hour.

- Store in a refrigerator in a sealed container for up to 5 days. Can be frozen and enjoyed for 1 month.

SEA SALTED CHOCOLATE FAT BOMBS

INGREDIENTS:

1/2 cup thick whipped cream

1 teaspoon of vanilla

1/2 cup of coconut oil

1/2 cup of sunflower butter

2 tablespoons cocoa powder

1/3 cup cream cheese

1 teaspoon of cinnamon

3 tablespoons herb butter

2 teaspoons of coarse sea salt

OPTIONAL:

Your favorite sugar substitute (I do not use a sugar substitute, once you're in the habit of not eating sugar, these are sweet enough without additives.)

NOTE:

These fat sea salt chocolate bombs are THE bomb and will help ketos in trouble and carbohydrate eaters low in dessert desires.

DIRECTIONS:

Step 1

Whisk whipping cream until soft peaks form, then add vanilla and stir.

2nd step

Place the sun butter, coconut oil, butter, cinnamon, cream cheese and cocoa powder in the bowl of a food processor and blend until smooth.

Step 3

Gently stir in the sunscreen mixture with the whipped cream.

Step 4

Pour the mixture into silicone molds, then sprinkle with coarse sea salt and freeze 6-8 hours or overnight.

Savoury Fat Bomb Recipes

KETO JALAPEÑO POPPERS FAT BOMBS

Ingredients

3.5 ounces whole cream cheese at room temperature, 100 g

1/4 cup unsalted butter or ghee at room temperature, 55g

4 slices no sugar bacon 120 g

1/4 cup Gruyere cheese or grated cheddar cheese 30 g

2 jalapeño peppers halved, seeded, and finely chopped, 29 g

US Customary - Metric

Instructions

- In a bowl, crush the cream cheese and butter or ghee, or pass to the robot to obtain a homogeneous mixture.

- Preheat oven to 160 ° C

- Line a baking sheet with parchment paper. Be sure to use a flanged sheet to hold the bacon fat, as you will also need it for the recipe.

- Lay the bacon slices flat on the parchment leaving enough space to prevent them from overlapping.

- Place the sheet in the preheated oven and cook for 25 to 30 minutes or until crisp. The exact duration of cooking depends on the thickness of the bacon slices.

- Take out of the oven and let them cool. When cooled, crumble bacon in a bowl and set aside.

- Add cheese with cream and butter, gruyere or cheddar, jalapeños and bacon fat. Mix well to combine. Refrigerate 30 minutes to 1 hour or until the mixture is firm

- Divide the mixture into 6 large bombs and place on a plate covered with parchment. If you serve them immediately, roll them in crumbled bacon until they are well coated. If you serve it later, refrigerate it without coating the bacon in an airtight container for up to 1 week. Roll large bombs in freshly cooked or heated bacon breadcrumbs just before serving.

Savory Salmon Fat Bombs

Ingredients (Makes 6 servings)

1/2 cup whole cream cheese (100 g / 3.5 oz)

1/3 cup butter, grass fed (75 g / 2.7 oz)

1/2 pack of smoked salmon or smoked mackerel (50 g / 1.8 oz)

1 tablespoon fresh lemon juice

1-2 tbsp freshly chopped dill soup (or 1 tbsp) - skip if using mackerel

to choose: pinch of salt (I love the pink Himalayas)

When looking for ingredients, try to get them in their most natural form (organic, without unnecessary additives).

Instructions

- Place the cream cheese, butter and smoked salmon in a food processor.

- Add fresh lemon juice and dill and beat until smooth. I use my Kenwood mixer with a food processor accessory.

- Line a tray of parchment paper and create small fat bombs using about 2 1/2 tablespoons of the mixture per piece. Garnish with more dill and refrigerate for 1-2 hours or until firm.

- You can also pour the mixture into an airtight container. Eat immediately or refrigerate for up to a week. When ready to serve, pour about 2 1/2 tablespoons per serving. M eat on crisp lettuce leaves or spread on Keto Ultimate Bread, Healthy Low-Carb Bagels or Low-Carb Rye Bread.

Baked Brie and Pecan Prosciutto Savory Fat Bombs

ingredients

1 slice of prosciutto, about ½ ounce

1 ounce of full fat Brie

6 halves of pecan, about an ounce

⅛ teaspoon of black pepper

Instructions

Preheat the oven to 350 ° F. Use a muffin pan with holes about 2.5 inches wide and 1.5 inches deep.

Take the slice of prosciutto and fold it in half so that it becomes almost square.

Place it in a hole in the muffin pan to align it completely.

Cut the brie into small cubes leaving the skin white. Place the brie in the cup lined with prosciutto.

Glue the pecan halves in the middle of Brie.

Bake for about 12 minutes, until the brie is melted and the prosciutto is cooked.

Let cool 10 minutes before leaving the muffin pan.

Breakfast Bacon Fat Bombs

Ingredients:

1 boiled egg

1/4 of lawyer

4 c. Soup unsalted or clarified butter

1 tablespoon mayonnaise

1 Serrano pepper, seeded and diced

1 tablespoon chopped coriander

Kosher salt to taste

Crushed pepper to your liking

Lime juice 1/4

2 tbsp. At the bacon fat table

6 slices of cooked bacon

Instructions:

In a large bowl, combine the hard-boiled egg, avocado, butter, mayonnaise, pepper serrano and coriander.

Crush into a smooth dough with a fork or rammer. Season with salt and pepper, then add lime juice and stir.

Prepare bacon in your favorite way until it is crisp, reserving 2 tablespoons of bacon fat. Add the bacon fat to the fat mixture and stir gently. Cover and refrigerate for 30 minutes or until mixture is cool and can form solid balls. Crumble the bacon into small pieces in a small bowl.

Using a spoon, take 6 equal amounts of the bomb mix and form balls. Add the bacon pellets and roll them until they are completely covered. Serve immediately.

Cheesy Pesto Fat Bombs

Ingredients

1 cup whole cream cheese (240 g)

2 tbsp. Basil Pesto (30 g / 1.1 oz) - you can prepare your own pesto

1/2 cup grated parmesan (45 g / 1.6 oz)

10 sliced olives (28 g / 1 oz)

Optional: salt and pepper to taste

Eat with:

Freshly cut cucumber slices, peppers or crisp lettuce leaves

Or refrigerate for 30 minutes, create dumplings and roll them into grated or crumbled parmesan cheese as i did in this mediterranean fat or bits of bacon crumbled like in my fat bacon and egg bombs.

Savory Pizza Fat Bombs

THE PREPARATION

4 ounces of cream cheese

14 slices of pepperoni

8 pitted black olives

2 tablespoons dried tomato pesto

2 tablespoons chopped fresh basil

Salt and pepper to taste

THE EXECUTION

- Cut the pepperoni and olives into small pieces.

- Combine basil, tomato pesto and cream cheese.

- Add the olives and pepperoni in the cream cheese and mix again.

- Form dumplings, then garnish with pepperoni, basil and olive.

That makes a total of 6 Pizza Fat Bombs. Each big bomb contains 101.33 calories, 9.62 grams of fat, 1.69 grams of net carbs and 2.26 grams of protein.

BACON, BRAUNSHWEIGER, & PISTACHIO TRUFFLES

INGREDIENTS:

8 oz Braunshweiger (Liverwurst), room temperature

1/4 cup chopped pistachio kernels

6 oz cream cheese, softened

1 teaspoon mustard dijon

8 slices of bacon, crunchy and finely chopped

INSTRUCTIONS:

Combine the Braunshweiger and pistachios in a small food processor and pulse.

In a small separate bowl, whisk cream cheese and mustard until smooth.

Roll the Braunshweiger in 12 small balls.

Then take each bale and form with your fingers a layer of cream cheese about 1/4 inch thick.

Once you're done, let it cool for about 30 minutes.

Roll each ball into finely chopped bacon and place on a serving platter.

Serve cold or at room temperature.

5 Cheese and Bacon Cauliflower Bites

INGREDIENTS:

5 cups Riced cauliflower

1 lb. bacon, cooked and crumbled

Cream cheese 8 oz - softened

4 oz. Goat cheese

1 1/2 cup grated parmesan cheese - divided

1/2 cup of strong cheddar cheese

1/2 cup white cheddar cheese with minced garlic

1 cup crushed pork rind

1/2 cup panko (to make gluten-free, replace panko with crushed pork rinds)

3 chopped garlic cloves

1 tsp Italian Seasoning- Divided

1 tsp Onion Powder

1 tsp Garlic powder

1/2 tsp Sea salt

1/2 tsp Black pepper

Oil

(2 Tbs. Peace and Love)

DIRECTIONS:

- To rice the cauliflower, you can beat it in a food processor or even just use a cheese grater. I used a cheese grater.

- In a large bowl, combine cauliflower, bacon, softened cream cheese, goat cheese, strong cheddar cheese, white cheddar cheese with garlic, 1/2 cup grated parmesan cheese, minced garlic, 1/2 tsp. Italian seasoning, sea salt and pepper. Mix until all ingredients are well incorporated. Refrigerate 1-2 hours to firm.

- Combine crushed pork rinds, remaining 1 cup Parmesan, Panko and 1 1/2 tbsp. Italian seasoning, onion powder and garlic powder. This mixture will be your breadcrumb.

Once the cauliflower mixture has had time to cool and harden, roll the mixture into uniform balls. I made mine about an inch and a half to two inches in diameter. That's 30 balls. Freeze for 3 hours, until night.

- In a large saucepan, heat about 1 inch of oil over medium-high heat. The use of different oils will change the temperature at which you should heat it. Be sure to check the smoke point for any oil you choose to use. When I fry things on the stove, I use my non-stick wok. The high sides help prevent splashing and make cleaning easier.

- Roll each ball into the mixture for breading until well coated. When the oil is beautiful and hot, drop the balls by 5 or 6 at a time. It will be obvious when it is time to return them. Fry until they are a beautiful golden brown everywhere.

- Remove from oil and cool on a paper towel. The paper towel will absorb the excess fat. I served them with a low carb marinara and a ranch vinaigrette. They both made great dips.

Savory Mediterranean Fat Bombs

Ingredients:

1/2 cup cream cheese, full-fat (100 g)

1/4 cup butter or ghee, softened at room temperature - you can make your own ghee (55 g)

2-3 tbsp At the table of freshly cut herbs (basil, thyme and oregano) or 2 tbsp. Dried herbs

4 pieces of sun-dried tomatoes, drained (12 g)

4 olives, pitted, kalamata or other (12 g)

2 cloves of garlic, crushed

freshly ground black pepper

1/4 tsp Salt tea or more to taste (I love the pink Himalayas)

5 tbsp Parmesan cheese, grated (25 g)

Instructions:

- Cut the butter into small pieces and place it in a bowl with the cream cheese. Leave it on a kitchen counter for 20-30 minutes to soften it. Crush with a fork and mix well. Add the dried tomatoes and chopped kalamata olives.

- Add freshly minced (or dried) herbs, crushed garlic and season with salt and pepper. Mix well and refrigerate for 20-30 minutes to solidify.

- Remove the cheese mixture from the refrigerator and start making 5 meatballs. You can use a spoon or ice cream scoop. Roll each ball into grated parmesan cheese and place on a plate. Eat immediately or refrigerate in an airtight container for up to a week.

www.ingramcontent.com/pod-product-compliance
Lightning Source LLC
Chambersburg PA
CBHW071447070526
44578CB00001B/253